An Educator's GPS

An Educator's GPS

Fending Off the Free Market of Schooling for America's Students

Jeff Swensson, John Ellis, and Michael Shaffer

ROWMAN & LITTLEFIELD
Lanham • Boulder • New York • London

Published by Rowman & Littlefield
An imprint of The Rowman & Littlefield Publishing Group, Inc.
4501 Forbes Boulevard, Suite 200, Lanham, Maryland 20706
www.rowman.com

6 Tinworth Street, London SE11 5AL

Copyright © 2019 by Jeff Swensson, John Ellis, and Michael Shaffer

All rights reserved. No part of this book may be reproduced in any form or by any electronic or mechanical means, including information storage and retrieval systems, without written permission from the publisher, except by a reviewer who may quote passages in a review.

British Library Cataloguing in Publication Information Available

Library of Congress Cataloging-in-Publication Data Available

ISBN: 978-1-4758-5078-9 (cloth)
ISBN: 978-1-4758-5079-6 (pbk.)
ISBN: 978-1-4758-5080-2 (electronic)

Contents

Introduction: On Behalf of America's Students — vii

1. Free Market Schooling Pushes Traditional Public Education Out on a Limb — 1
2. Why Bother with Self-Defense? We're Busy Enough Already! — 5
3. What Are Traditional Public Educators Defending? — 15
4. Staking a Claim on the Primary Purpose of Traditional Public Education — 21
5. In Defense of Traditional Public Education: Intelligence and Thinking — 29
6. In Defense of Traditional Public Education: Function — 39
7. What Happens When Educators Teach *How to Think*? — 49
8. How Do Traditional Public Educators Know That Self-Defense Is Necessary? — 59
9. Don't Say You Weren't Warned! The Dangers of Free Market Schooling — 63
10. Mediated Identity in Windows and Mirrors — 69
11. The Context of Free Market Testing Invokes a Culture of Failure — 89
12. Tales, Stories, Fables, and Myths in the Free Market — 109
13. Policymaking: Is That a Light at the End of the Tunnel? — 125
14. The Self-Defense Responsibilities of Traditional Public Educators — 137

References — 149
Index — 159
About the Authors — 161

Introduction

On Behalf of America's Students

All of America's students are the centerpiece of this book. On behalf of students throughout the United States, this book is organized around the data, research, professional practice, and quality instruction in comprehensive traditional public education that fend off the deficits inherent in free market schooling. This dynamic discussion of traditional public education illustrates why a defense of this perspective is required to ensure the delivery of bright futures to all US students.

A stalwart defense of traditional public education in the United States is required because political and policymaking perspectives aligned with the free market of schooling (also referred to as *privatization* or *choice schooling*) at both the state and national levels are designed to destroy traditional public schools. This book shares the efforts of proponents of free market ideology to defund, deconstruct, and delimit the important positive impact of traditional public education in its service to all of America's children and young people.

This book is organized around details about the free market of schooling that are little known and rarely acknowledged by adherents. Details about free market theory and the strategies that implement this perspective reveal how policymakers, plutocrats, and politicians intend to transform each state's most expensive budgetary item into a less expensive fixed expenditure without regard to the quality of the service rendered and without investment in oversight to ensure positive student-centered outcomes. This book is organized around ideas about quality instruction and a primary purpose for traditional public education that serve to defend the teaching and learning that 90 percent of America's students experience every day. This book is organized around strategies that traditional public educators can apply to advance the learning of every student. This book is organized to share, illustrate, and advocate so that traditional public education continues to be America's best service on behalf of all students.

ONE

Free Market Schooling Pushes Traditional Public Education Out on a Limb

This book is a response to the impossible situation familiar to traditional public educators throughout the United States. A chasm between two prominent perspectives about teaching and learning confounds the purpose of education in America.

Free market theory supports and promotes one of these perspectives: choice education, also known as *privatization*. The second major perspective is traditional public education. This chapter begins a dialogue devoted to defending traditional public education because proponents of free market schooling push US traditional public education out on a limb.

Although free market schooling enrolls barely 10 percent of students in the United States, policymakers, networks, individuals, and politicians support an aggressive and well-funded attempt to establish a free market agenda for schooling via mechanisms like vouchers, charter schools, and tax credits. Replacing and eliminating traditional public education, free market theory prioritizes less government and lower taxes instead of teaching and learning.

The purpose of this chapter is to describe free market theory and its relationship with American schooling. This knowledge is critical to the thinking and actions required to bring traditional public education in the United States off the limb.

ATTRIBUTES OF FREE MARKET THINKING

Free market theory "'denies the importance of public goods or else maintains that all our goods are best achieved by individuals acting out of individual self-interest'" (Hostetler, 2003, p. 355). Claims about the beneficence created by free market schooling camouflage survival of the fittest funded by massive amounts of cash. Choice schooling drowns educational adequacy in a storm of social Darwinism.

The choices offered in the free market, furthermore, foster nothing less than educational apartheid. Proponents of the free market of schooling in the United States—referred to throughout this discussion as *marketeers*—promote choice as if it's available to all students and their families. In the free market, however, school choice is restricted.

Among the paradoxes visited upon teaching and learning in the United States by free market proponents is the restriction of choice that accompanies the article of faith delivered by free market theory that less government for less cost is the best government. Even though regulations, taxes, statutes, and rules are aspects of government allied with traditional public education that constitute the antithesis of free market theory, marketeers have few qualms in putting the policymaking and legislative fiat to work to advance choice schooling enrollment restrictions and funding practices.

Traditional public education, from the perspective of free market theory, is a burden and an overreach because government intrudes on what rightly belongs to individuals—wealth, freedom, choice—when it mandates school attendance and when it collects taxes in support of traditional public education.

SCHOOLING IN THE FREE MARKET

Marketeers are dedicated to the belief "that schools (public sector) should be run like businesses (private sector), [which] while lacking any evidentiary warrant, has become a new 'common sense' among a wide swath of the American public (Cuban, 2004; Goodsell, 2004; Mautner, 2010)" (Anderson and Donchik, 2016, p. 337). These agenda priorities of free market proponents constitute the characteristics of schooling that marketeers call *reform*.

The agenda of the free market aims to install choice education that is "concerned less with measuring whether schools help students learn and more with whether parents have an opportunity to pick a school for their children" (Brown, 2017). The threat to traditional public education represented by choice schooling becomes more ominous when the ballyhooed advantages of free market schooling primarily benefit adults instead of students.

THREATS, TRADITIONAL PUBLIC EDUCATION, AND THE FREE MARKET

Traditional public education colleagues prioritize identifying and dealing with threats to student safety because thinking thrives in safe learning environments. In the same way that fire drills represent this long-standing dedication to student safety, anti-drug efforts, bullying-prevention programs, and lockdown drills illustrate the new normal for student safety. Over time, traditional public education colleagues—with a special tip of the cap to school resource officers—improved the number and sophistication of drills and practices that are the bedrock of a safe learning environment.

The safe learning environments that students deserve also account for threats that arise from unmet student needs. Many of these needs are addressed meaningfully by at-school social work and guidance counseling professionals.

When student needs eclipse the professional expertise of public educators, collaboration with medical and dental providers, charitable groups, governmental agencies, and a variety of community or service organizations addresses threats in students' lives that short-circuit their attention to learning *how to think*.

The response of one school to Tina, a sixth-grade student, symbolizes how the practice of traditional public education involves the activation of collaborative resources in pursuit of student well-being and the primary purpose of traditional public education.

STUDENT SNAPSHOT: TINA

A quiet, diminutive, young lady, Tina moved into our school district at the start of the school year. The threats to Tina's well-being came to colleagues' attention quickly. Both a custodian and a teacher on lunch duty observed Tina asking other students for uneaten food. She wrapped it in napkins and put the food in her pockets. Tina discretely pulled apples and bananas out of the trash.

The custodian and the teacher informed Tina's guidance counselor and the school social worker. The multiple interventions undertaken in concert with outside social agencies (often referred to as wrap-around services) were called into play. After a home visit from our social worker and Tina's lead team teacher, Tina and her family were engaged by a variety of different programs. Medical and dental check-ups were arranged at a local clinic.

The community center serving Tina's neighborhood enrolled her in afterschool care and connected the family with a local food pantry. Tina's mother enrolled in job training at the center. At school, the federal Free/Reduced Lunch Program was operationalized immediately.

Tina's counselor talked with her regularly and made sure that teachers were in the loop so that effective support for learning was in place throughout her three years in our school. By the time Tina left for her freshman year at our high school, her grades, her physical well-being, her interactions with peers, and her prospects for a fulfilling future were robust.

THE THREAT FROM THE FREE MARKET

These numerous threats to America's students—violence, homelessness, poverty—are squarely on the radar of traditional public education colleagues. But traditional public education is out on a limb because too little attention is paid to the threat represented by free market theory.

The adult-centric focus of the free market for schooling goes largely unchallenged. Emphasizing the implementation of mechanisms (e.g., charter schools, vouchers, tax credits), adherents of the free market assault traditional public education, its purpose, its quality, and its outcomes. When choice education adherents seek the realization of free market goals rooted in a theory usually allied with economics and politics, the learning future of US students is undermined.

The free market hypothesized by privatization adherents, for instance, forswears regulation with the promise of greater freedom for individuals. The result is that existing guarantees of equity and equality found in traditional public education often no longer apply to students enrolled in choice schooling.

For example, schooling fostered by free market theory puts children at risk because "when students use vouchers to get into private school, they lose most of the protections of the federal Individuals with Disabilities Education Act" (Goldstein, 2017). This loss is compounded because, in choice schools, students often give up the added protection of having a teacher who has specialized in teaching students with an IEP.

Paradoxically, this is good news from the perspective of proponents of free market schooling. Reducing the size of government and its tax burden happens when the number of children served by government-mandated programs is reduced. Even better news for marketeers is that government funding can be manipulated to cover the costs of implementing and sustaining state support for free market schooling mechanisms.

The threat presented to US students by free market schooling goes largely unnoticed because the focus of traditional public educators is squarely on the well-being of students and the value of the primary purpose of traditional public education. Without adequate resources and without sufficient time to pay attention to anything but students, colleagues offer little in the way of resistance while moneyed interests favoring the free market drive privatization forward and push traditional public education out on a limb.

TWO

Why Bother with Self-Defense? We're Busy Enough Already!

Traditional public school colleagues already have more than enough to do. In an era when traditional public schools are the only functioning civic organization in the lives of many US families—apart from the US Post Office—is it necessary to talk about self-defense strategies for public school education?

After all, because traditional US public schools serve not only a primary purpose but also provide a multitude of social services—health care provision, food/clothing distribution, child care centers before and after school hours, military recruiting centers at the high school level, public shelters in times of community emergencies, community/neighborhood identity—wouldn't it be a reasonable assumption that traditional public schools and all who serve in them are held in high regard throughout society?

TIRED? YOU BET!

Sadly, the fact is that too little regard is paid to the essential and effective work done throughout traditional public schools in the United States. Instead of plaudits, traditional public educators are assailed by free market advocates who rail against "a rule-laden, risk-averse sector dominated by entrenched bureaucracies, industrial style collective-bargaining agreements, and hoary colleges of education" (Hess, 2010, p. 47).

In response, the discussion throughout this book speaks without hesitation to the fact that traditional public educators are tired of being the punching bag for moneyed and ideological perspectives. Fueled by dismay with dismissive name-calling and self-righteous bombast from free market adherents, traditional public educators have data and research that confirms the abiding value of traditional public education and that constitutes the foundation for self-defense presented throughout this book.

It's time for colleagues to rally; it's time to examine, discuss, and defend against free market theory and its disservice to teaching and learning in the United States.

FOUR SELF-DEFENSE FACTORS

Four factors initiate this discussion about the need to defend traditional public education in the United States. These four set the stage for defending traditional public education with what's best for teaching, learning, and US students.

1. *Public education's primary purpose* is to teach all students *how to think*. This purpose is critical to the success that students deserve because, as researchers illustrate, "the brain is not hardwired but plastic, mutable, something that reorganizes itself with each new task" (Brown, Roediger, and McDaniel, 2014, p. 166).

    Public education colleagues have the opportunity and responsibility to employ the neuroplasticity of the brain to engage all students in building the cognitive structures and behaviors required for cognitive agency, which facilitates the capability to choose a balance between individual and public goods in US democracy.

2. *The practice of traditional public education*—all the daily decisions and behaviors of colleagues—advances *how to think* either directly or indirectly.

    To create the most positive impact possible on the cognition of all students, it's necessary for traditional public education colleagues to craft and apply knowledge and cognition process about the nature of thinking and intelligence. Applying what is known about thinking and intelligence fuels the development in professional practice of ways to organize, prioritize, and teach *habits of mind*, also known as thinking skills.

3. *The attack on public education* is extremely serious. Free market proponents intend to destroy traditional US public education. If educators fail to mount a defense against this insidious assault, the lived experience of all students, social justice, the American Dream, and the public good are in peril.

4. *Traditional public educators* neither understand nor identify effectively the origins of the free market of schooling. They do not perceive accurately the free market ideology and the my-side bias at the foundation of privatization.

These four self-defense factors are the baseline for an awareness that traditional public educators must develop if the purpose and quality in their professional practice are to have an impact worthy of all of America's students and their futures. Traditional public educators are tired of the charade perpetrated by free marketeers. Those who offer this charade—that free market schooling is America's better source of innovative instruction, superior academic results, and low-cost government-free efficiencies—must be confronted by traditional public educators with data about the quality for students that their professional practice represents.

WHAT DOES THE FREE MARKET CHARADE LOOK LIKE?

Like shadows on the wall of a cave, claims made in the name of free market theory are unreliable. Fables, denials, gimmicks, myths, impressions, and shenanigans fostered by proponents claim that a free market of schooling is required to avoid the supposed missteps of traditional public education. These are alluring, but misleading, representations of the nature and impact of choice education.

Mechanisms—vouchers, charter schools, tax credits, and education savings accounts—are the heart of schooling implemented through free market theory. Via mechanisms, free market theory "equates the political man with the economic man, arguing that policymakers create laws as if they were competitors in an open market, choosing options that preserve their status over those which generate the most public good (Kelman, 1987)" (Dawkins-Law, 2014, p. 2).

Choice schooling proponents advance mechanisms as both the means and the ends of schooling in the United States. This means that understanding mechanisms means understanding free market schooling and its impact on America's students. A successful defense of traditional public education is rooted in a thorough knowledge of the intents and outcomes of choice education.

INTRODUCING FREE MARKET SCHOOLING

It is not possible to introduce free market schooling and data at the same time. This is the case because data of any kind—particularly research that compares the academic proficiency of traditional public schools with achievement in choice schools—gains little traction with, and causes no self-reflection among, proponents of privatization. Data, however, reveals the problems, oxymorons, pitfalls, and dangers of free market schooling.

Academic Proficiency Data

Numerous studies over the past two decades find "that private schools, with or without vouchers, do not improve the education provided to a community's children (National Center for Educational Statistics, 2006)" (Covaleskie, 2007, p. 34). Those most in need of the social justice of equality and *how to think* are isolated by the very nature of privatization.

Anemic academic performance locked into the context of privatization is an outcome of free market schooling across the United States. In Michigan, for instance, observers relate that the implementation of choice schooling is not about education but about business profit (Binelli, 2017). In Louisiana, including New Orleans, privatization funded by the Louisiana Scholarship Program (LSP) shifts "students into lower performance categories and increase[s] the likelihood of failing scores" (Abdulkadiroglu, Pathak, and Walters, 2015, p. 9).

Free market schooling in Ohio offers nothing better, where data about student academic performance from the Cleveland Scholarship and Tutoring Program shows that "the test score gain for voucher recipients was significantly lower in math and reading than for applicants who were not offered a voucher" (Rouse and Barrow, 2008, p. 19).

Data from Standardized Testing

Among the misdirections fostered by free market schooling proponents is the stance that standardized testing is a valuable barometer for determining academic proficiency and is only relevant if it's used to imply that only traditional public education delivers less than stellar achievement outcomes for its students.

Allegations about low test scores in traditional public education are raised to insinuate the efficiencies of free market schooling into the dialogue. Instead of inspiring conversation about the valueless nature of standardized testing, proponents of free market schooling share negative impressions about achievement in traditional public education without acknowledging similar, or lower, standardized scores earned in free market schools. In this way, "these scores, which formerly were predictors of more interesting criteria, have now become criteria, or ends, in themselves" (Sternberg, Reznitskaya, and Jarvin, 2007, p. 156).

It is paradoxical, at least, that privatization proponents dwell upon information about bureaucracy-infused, lower order cognition-dependent examinations when criticizing traditional public education. Worse, however, is that this preoccupation with testing lower order cognitive skills confirms that marketeers are oblivious to, and disdainful of, a primary purpose in free market schooling: to engage all students with quality instruction.

Instead of *how to think*, free market advocates embrace context, the mechanisms of the free market, as the purpose of schooling.

Data about Fiscal Impact

Free market schooling, empowered by legislation that aids and abets mechanisms, is nothing less than the reallocation of funds from state budgets originally meant to finance traditional public education.

The dire fiscal impact of free market theory on traditional public educators is revealed in data analyzed in the late teens of this century. This data revealed that, "nationally, teacher pay is 1.6 percent below their average earnings in 1999 and five percent lower than their 2009 pay, adjusted for inflation, according to the Department of Education" (Picchi, 2018).

Data about Societal Impacts

In Milwaukee (the home of the first charter school system in the United States [Turner, 2016]), learning-disabled students are far less likely to be enrolled in choice schooling than students in the city's traditional public schools (Fleming et al., 2013). Students enrolled in virtual charter schools in Indiana (home of the largest voucher system in the nation) earn low scores on the state's standardized test while charter schools in the capital city, Indianapolis, "are some of the city's most segregated" (Donheiser, 2017).

Except for their devotion to reporting the number of, and total enrollment in, free market schools, marketeers abandon data-based sharing about the effect of mechanisms on the learning and lives of America's students. Moreover, points of view that do not align with the primacy of self-interest manipulated in the market are ignored by marketeers when policy, practice, and politics at the core of choice schooling are formulated.

The self-serving nature of free market theory at the foundation of privatization and the dollars expended to implement schooling aligned with this theory are among the reasons the time has come for traditional public education colleagues to forge a defensive alliance with data.

AN ELEGANT TRUTH ABOUT TEACHING AND LEARNING

This discussion is anchored by an elegant truth about teaching and learning: "It is not enough to simply consume predigested knowledge, one must also become a knowledge builder (Scandamalia, Bereiter, & Lamon, 1994) and problem solver (Polya, 1957; Schoenfeld, 1982; Selz, 1935)" (Ritchart and Perkins, 2005, p. 777). This defense of traditional public education relies on an understanding that if human beings are not taught *how to think*, the result is the entrenchment of a narrow self-centered cognition.

Traditional public education at its best—in the past, for the present, and into the future—follows this elegant truth in every professional interaction to yield an education during which all students learn *how to think*. Traditional public education colleagues are in perpetual motion, cognitively speaking, on behalf of this primary purpose. Classroom instruction, conversations about appropriate behavior, directions for completing a homework assignment, evaluation of written assignments—all symbolize the large and small ways in which traditional public educators pursue *how to think* for all students each day.

A compelling interest in creating the conditions necessary and sufficient for learning *how to think* demands a comparison between traditional public education and free market schooling. Traditional public education is nothing less than the essential bulwark against schooling for incomplete, limited, self-aggrandizing choosing. Defending a primary purpose offers a necessary pushback against free market schooling and its negative impact.

A Gift Rejected in Favor of Free Market Objectives

Quality instruction in traditional public education in the United States engages all students in the baseline dimensions for *how to think* that emerge from Bloom's Taxonomy and its revision: knowledge and cognitive process (Bloom, 1956; Krathwohl, 2002). Initiating *how to think* with these dimensions at the foundation of choices of professional practice *leads out* to higher order cognitive behaviors when traditional public educators invest in what will be referred to in this discussion as *function*.

Function and *how to think*, however, have no value in the free market. The wide-ranging and comprehensive explorations of ideas and experiences (curricular, co-curricular, and extracurricular) created in quality comprehensive traditional public education are a "gift of the kind of education that we no longer value" (Lithwick, 2018).

The free market has no interest in and no room for "the kind of 1950s-style public education that has all but vanished in America and that is being dismantled with great deliberation as funding for things like the arts, civics, and enrichment are zeroed out" (Lithwick, 2018). The gift of comprehensive traditional public education is exchanged for mechanisms and the objectives sought by free market schooling.

Data from Indiana in 2017, for instance, provides a glimpse into objectives linked to free market schooling and its mechanisms. In the Hoosier State, enrollment in the $150 million-per-year voucher program is increasingly White and affluent; more than 50 percent of these voucher students never attended any public school (Colombo, 2017).

Less government and a concomitant reduction of taxes are fundamental objectives of free market theory. Realized through budgetary reductions that affect vocational and technical education offered in comprehensive traditional public education, these objectives are pursued frequently at the federal level.

For instance, frequent and intense efforts by legislative allies of comprehensive traditional public education are necessary year after year to preserve funding for the Perkins Act ("the federal law governing roughly $1 billion in spending each year on career and technical training" [Stratford, 2018a]). The depth and extent of the persistence of advocates of free market schooling to foster less government creates legislative battles like this that students in comprehensive public education cannot fight but can lose.

The Inelegance of Market Purity: Context as Mechanisms

From time to time throughout this book, *that* traditional public education colleague (everyone knows at least one) who is extremely good at connecting professional practice with the theoretical or conceptual foundations of ideas and practices will enter the discussion.

For now, *that* colleague comes into the dialogue to introduce a profound concern surrounding free market schooling: privatization is about context. The dialectic between fundamental stability and changing emergent that signifies a healthy organization (Poole and van de Ven, 1989) is missing from the context, the mechanisms, at the core of free market schooling.

Schooling rendered in the name of the free market constitutes teaching and learning inertia. Composed of a multitude of pretenses—for example, choice theory benefits everyone because mechanisms endow choice with efficiency and freedom—the context of choice schooling is derived from, and dependent upon, the stasis of market purity.

The stability of context proclaimed by privatization proponents wobbles when data appears. For instance, almost 25 percent of charter school teachers turn over each year, more than two times the rate of teacher departures in traditional public schools (Kahlenberg and Potter, 2014).

The changing emergent of free market schooling is symbolized in the belief that closing inefficient charter schools at any point in a school year is efficient. But this centerpiece of choice schooling leaves students and their families without the stability of recourse to a replacement institution. Free market schooling enrollees and their families become subject to what we will refer to as *stealth-schooling*.

THE MOVEMENT THAT IS STEALTH-SCHOOLING*

This book is dedicated to exposing the dangerous failures of privatization and stealth-schooling, where context and self-aggrandizement bury *how to think*. Self-defense is necessary because privatization produces nothing less than a slow-moving nationwide calamity for student achievement and US democracy. Put simply, "privatization represents *movement* towards private or individual models of control" (Lubienski, 2013, p. 502).

[*Authors' clarification: *Some privatization proponents and homeschoolers proudly indicate that choice schools stealthily take schooling away from traditional public education and place it in an alternative or home setting. They refer to this self-proclaimed reform as "stealth schooling." Our premise is that privatization, and its focus on mechanisms and the implementation of a free market dedicated to adult-centric objectives is stealthy only in the sense that this focus obscures and denigrates the quality teaching and learning necessary to the futures of all US students. Throughout this book, the term* stealth-schooling *is used to convey the duplicitous and damaging outcomes masquerading as reform within the promotion and exercise of free market schooling.*]

For free market advocates, reform occurs when mechanisms facilitate choice, competition, the primacy of self-interest, and efficiency. At the core of these alleged reforms of teaching and learning lies a significant problem that must be accounted for when defending traditional public education. Marketeers "increasingly cast public schools in formalist terms—categorizing them by their form, rather than their function—while trimming those terms to better align with their own structure" (Stitzlein, 2017).

For US students, *how to think* is not a matter of form. *How to think* is not realized through mechanisms created to reduce both cost and the size of government. In comprehensive traditional public education, instead, US students engage with instructional practices fueled by function on a cognitive journey destined to maximize successful intelligence for all.

Free market schooling proponents, on the other hand, assume that context is purpose. Mechanisms ensure that the exclusionary proposition aligned with objectives of free market theory takes center stage. This key proposition of free market theory is that success is not possible for everyone.

Embracing this proposition, unregulated free market mechanisms sort and restrict who attends choice schools. Because "private schools are better able to select and retain students they believe will succeed in their program" (Cowen et al., 2013, p. 164), enrollment practices are the day-to-day implementation of the exclusionary proposition and its embrace of the choices mired in the predilections, prejudices, or privileges of free market-favored families. Mechanisms are context in a marketplace where segregation and on-the-cheap professional practice are manipulated by marketeers.

These, and other, context-embedded outcomes of stealth-schooling are deliberate. Well-established networks, foundations, and institutes (whose participants include, among others, the American Legislative Exchange Council [ALEC], the Fordham Institute, the Institute for Justice [DeBray-Pelot, Lubienski, and Scott, 2007], the Lynde and Harry Bradley Foundation, and the Walton Family Foundation [Bielke, 2017]) provide ample financial support and generate copious printed material to foster the outcomes of free market schooling.

John Dewey seemed to anticipate the pernicious impact of these characteristics of free market schooling on America when he wrote that "the essential point is that isolation makes for rigidity and formal institutionalizing of life, for static and selfish ideals within the group" (Dewey, 1916, p. 40).

Traditional public education colleagues need to understand that when free market adherents make promises about privatization, each such assertion must be taken with an iceberg-sized grain of salt. Stealth-schooling and its context contravene function in traditional public education through outcomes that are relevant only to true believers in the primacy of self-interest.

This movement toward private/individual models of control pushes the nation toward a model for schooling that unabashedly serves selected and privileged cohorts of US citizens. Excluded and isolated by the mechanisms of privatization, most US students are cognitively and socially disenfranchised by free market schooling.

THE NECESSITY OF SELF-DEFENSE

Somewhere along the way, a unified professional perspective about the primary purpose of comprehensive traditional public education got lost. This loss is reflected in the wayward interventions of the US Congress and US Department of Education in traditional public education. This loss is manifest in the state-by-state politicization of traditional public education via marketplace-aligned statutory fiat. This loss is reflected in the relative reserve of traditional public educators when it comes to messaging about purpose and quality. These losses help push professional practice in traditional public education further out on a limb.

Loss is established when the nature of student achievement is consigned to the status of a great unknown; in searching numerous free market–aligned statutes and rules promulgated across legislative and regulatory entities, it's not possible to find a clear definition of student achievement. Unfortunately, traditional public educators battle among themselves over the different purposes of professional practice. The result is that the mysteries and myopic analyses of standardized testing become the imprecision and misdirection of the US conversation about academic proficiency.

The result of this confusion is that policymakers are left to make up their own best guess about the purpose of teaching and learning. With so many of these leaders transfixed by the siren song of the free market, when likeminded marketeers proclaim the self-aggrandizing benefits of free market schooling that are calculated with the results of standardized testing, policy for privatization follows close behind.

Isolation and static ideals espoused by privatization—efficiency, individual wealth, profit, and mechanisms—constitute a self-fulfilling prophecy when these ideals are the outcomes or the context used to substantiate the excellence of choice schools (Abdulkadiroglu, Pathak, and Walters, 2015). In the promotion of these characteristics of schooling, free market advocates forsake student achievement and the pursuit of *how to think*. Instead of forging a clear pathway designed to engage all students in academic proficiency, free market schooling obstructs the route to higher order cognition for 90 percent of US students.

THREE
What Are Traditional Public Educators Defending?

In response to the free market, its mechanisms, and privatization, traditional public education offers a primary purpose and quality instruction for all US students. A defense of these aspects of traditional public education is a defense of professional practice dedicated to valorizing the assets—lived experience, cognitive capacities, and successful intelligence—that all of America's students bring to school every day.

The defense of traditional public education entails the defense of an additional four allied constructs. Traditional public education does not exist in isolation within US society. The purpose and outcomes of traditional public education are connected to democracy, the cognitive intersection of science and art, covenant/attachment, and balance. Defending these constructs is an encounter with the greater good, of which traditional public education is an essential component.

IN DEFENSE OF DEMOCRACY

An understanding of the unbreakable bond between traditional public education and democracy in the United States owes a great deal to John Dewey, who observed more than a century ago that "the devotion of democracy to education is a familiar fact" (1916, p. 41). Although democracy and traditional public education are and ought to be inseparable, any traditional public educator's experiences reveal that this conjunction is not universally appreciated.

Proponents of privatization seek to separate democracy and traditional public education through the implementation of mechanisms that disconnect individuals from the promise in their own futures enhanced by *how to think*. This separation and the ascendency of mechanisms over academic achievement traps students in a context laden with my-side bias and thinking-as-rejection.

The anemic uninstructed cognition and woebegone academic results created by free market schooling reveal why, for millennia, human beings are not content with the cognitive restrictions of natural thinking. Education (rooted in the Latin, *educere*, to *lead out*) is all about leading human beings out of the restrictions inherent in natural thinking. Democracy, in the same way, is all about engaging human beings beyond autocracy. *Leading out*, therefore, contends against restrictions that forestall balance between individual and public goods.

When traditional public educators *lead out*, or educate, higher level cognition emerges as one important outcome of *how to think*. Exemplifying the conjunction of knowledge and cognitive process in evaluation, analysis, and creativity, effective pursuit of this primary purpose has long been a part of traditional public education and is symbolized by results earned on College Board Advanced Placement exams.

With more than a million US students taking these exams, educators are presented with one demonstration of the conjunction of traditional public education and higher order cognition. Young people earning a score of three or higher—the benchmark at which many colleges and universities grant college credit—increased by almost 70 percent between 2007 and 2017 (Stratford, 2018b). The practice of traditional public education *leads out* to habits of mind via instruction invested in definitions of thinking and learning, knowledge about the brain and intelligence, and understanding the meaning of balance and wisdom.

To defend democracy, traditional public education and its primary purpose align with the observation that "efforts to teach thinking do not simply target the here and now: They mean to serve the there and then" (Ritchart and Perkins, 2005, p. 788). Deep and broad learning for all students is the outcome of greatest value to democracy because this outcome embodies the fundamental moral purpose of US public education (Fullan, 2001; Hargreaves and Fink, 2004; Leo and Wickenberg, 2013).

This moral purpose embraces social justice, and social justice is a universal truth in democracy when and if the balance between individual and public goods arises via cognitive agency that results from the focus of comprehensive traditional public education on *how to think*.

IN DEFENSE OF SCIENCE AND ART

The professional practice of comprehensive traditional public education is both art and science. Compelling research and scholarship (Brown, Roediger, and McDaniel, 2014; Eisner, 1979; Lee, 1974; Lezotte and McKee, 2002; Marzano, 2007; Schmoker, 2006) convey the power and potential of this conceptual and practical intersection. The instruction that occurs in this intersection has been referenced as a mosaic of teaching choices and options (Dunbar, 2018).

Art and science mingle not only when educators select among research-based best practices to write curriculum and create lessons (Seaman, 2011) but also when quality instruction engages students in learning cognitive behaviors or thinking skills (these will be referenced in this book as *habits of mind*) during the journey toward *how to think*.

There is no intention in this overview to provide a template for professional practice in traditional public education; art and science do not interplay best as the replication of a recipe. Rather, traditional public education practices are all about the admixture of science and art that nurtures the capacities of each student that are necessary and sufficient for learning the cognitive "mosaic" of *how to think*.

The ideas, strategies, concepts, information, and data at the core of quality professional practices assume that colleagues will themselves create a mosaic of select research-based instruction, data-infused perspectives, theory-generated strategies, and/or amalgams of instructional practices that pursue the primary purpose of traditional public education for all students. This mosaic activity is referred to throughout this book as *function*.

The professional acumen of traditional public education colleagues emerges in a myriad of higher order cognitive behaviors. Selecting and applying quality instruction that yields *how to think* for all students is the demanding, difficult, work that is the art and science of our profession. The demands upon and the professionalism within day-to-day implementation of science and art in the practice of traditional public education is captured in an analogy suggested by Quinn (1989):

> If a doctor, lawyer, or dentist had 40 people in his office at one time, all of whom had different needs, and some of whom didn't want to be there, and were causing trouble, and the doctor, lawyer, or dentist, without assistance, had to treat them all with professional excellence for nine months, then he might have some conception of the classroom teacher's job.

The clear articulation of the art and science of practice in traditional public education is the self-defense through which privatization's dead ends are revealed and upended.

IN DEFENSE OF ATTACHMENT

Service as a traditional public education colleague exemplifies attachment and its value. Attachments that form us, but that we do not choose, include family, ethnic group, community, nation, and faith. Referred to as *covenantal attachments*, these explain "how humans are formed by relationships early in life, and are given the tools to go out and lead their lives" (Brooks, 2017).

Covenantal attachments are among the assets that all students bring to classrooms. And, as educators' professional experiences reveal, covenantal attachments are among the outcomes that attend *how to think*. *How to think* puts each student as a future voter into a reciprocal relationship with covenant in the sense that cognitive behaviors acquired along the journey toward *how to think* (responsive cognition and cognitive agency) establish the capacity for continuous improvement of democracy and the covenant it symbolizes for all people in the United States.

Democracy in the United States (attended by capitalism, transformative concepts anchoring liberty for all, and innumerable promises of freedom necessary for individual rights in American society) is a beneficiary of traditional public education. The role of the primary purpose of traditional public education is to engage individual cognitive capacities to the point that they are capable of choosing cognitive behaviors that balance individual good and the public good.

The public good is realized in the balance between individual freedoms and covenantal attachment. Without professional practice that *leads out* to create and sustain the cognitive agency that permits balance, imbalance between covenant and individual freedom arises. Detachment results when balance is absent. Disconnected, "freedom without covenant becomes selfishness," and "freedom without connection becomes alienation" (Brooks, 2017).

Self-defense strategies are necessary if traditional public educators are to fend off the detachment evinced in free market thinking. Privatization relies upon an every-man-for-himself approach to thinking, teaching, and learning nourished by selfishness and disconnection.

Traditional public education colleagues accept the difficult responsibility of crafting thinking suitable for a balance between attachment and freedom. The primary purpose of traditional public education puts teachers and learners in position to establish this dialectical relationship, which is essential to American democracy.

Balance between attachments (including the covenants of community and national obligations) and freedoms (fostered by liberty and individual rights guaranteed by American institutions) gives democracy the initiative and momentum required for continuous improvement of social justice, equality, and other promises of the American Dream. Detachment and alienation, on the other hand, thrive in the domain of privatization, where the primacy of individual rights profoundly disrupts the capacity for covenant and the creation of balance, required for the success of US democracy.

IN DEFENSE OF BALANCE

Balance between individual and public goods is the high-wire act necessary for the successful American democracy. Because this discussion invests in a definition of thinking as the transformation of mental representations of knowledge, the case is made that US democracy requires that these "manipulations must be systemic transformations governed by certain constraints" (Holyoak and Morrison, 2005, p. 2).

For traditional public education colleagues, these constraints are the sociocultural framework established by the public good, the sociocultural baseline of American democracy. Pursuing *how to think* as both necessary and sufficient to balancing individual and public goods puts traditional public educators in a position where a balance within professional practice is required.

Balanced professional practice is about teaching and learning that combines knowledge and cognitive process. Engaging students in lessons that access knowledge and cognition is maximized by the application of transformative learning theory.

Transformative learning theory provides a platform from which instructional behaviors congruent with our primary purpose can be launched. Elements of this theory that fuel professional practice on the journey toward *how to think* include "individual experience, critical reflection, dialogue, holistic orientation, context, and authentic relationships (Taylor, 2009)" (English and Irving, 2012, p. 250).

Incorporating these elements during lessons gives learners the ability to "move toward a frame of reference that is more inclusive, discriminating, self-reflective, and integrative of experience" (Mezirow, 1997, p. 5). Transformative learning theory is a point of contact with the cognitive behaviors, habits of mind, and actions that constitute wisdom.

Sternberg, Reznitskaya, and Jarvin (2007) observe that "wise thinking involves the ability to use one's intelligence in the service of a common good by balancing one's own interests with those of other people and of a broader community over both the short- and long-terms" (p. 150). *Leading-out* to engage this frame of reference and fulfill public education's moral purpose not only fulfills the promise of US democracy and the American Dream but also requires defense of science and art, attachment/covenant, democracy, and balance.

FOUR
Staking a Claim on the Primary Purpose of Traditional Public Education

During the past five decades, the authors of this book served as three individuals among the almost four million traditional public education colleagues in the United States (Green, E., 2018). The responsibilities of traditional public education colleagues for the learning and futures of all students is manifest in countless daily decisions and activities ranging from the heavily academic to the relatively mundane. Somewhere in between the bookends of daily responsibilities are countless hours spent on bus duty.

Standing bus duty at the start or the end of a school year during relatively balmy Midwestern weather encourages conversation with students and reflections among colleagues about the many positive characteristics of traditional public education. If only bus duty weather was always that glorious! But, rain, sleet, snow, wind, and bitter cold—the winter and early spring weather that seems glued to the start or end of each school day—encourages different thinking as the buses roll. When the weather is blustery and everyone hurries to unload or load the buses, gloomy weather becomes the backdrop for considering the origin and growth of multiple assaults on traditional public education and its primary purpose.

During the careers of the three authors, the assault on traditional public education emanated most often from the state chamber of commerce, the media, and key state legislators. Although the three authors started their careers in different locations with different teaching assignments, it was apparent everywhere that traditional public education faced significant resistance. The intensity of this animosity was, at first, surprising, and with time, alarming.

FALLING FLAT ALONGSIDE THE RESPONSE

To reverse the perceptions held, and outcomes generated, by detractors of traditional public education, the three authors and their colleagues collaborated on a variety of responses with uneven degrees of success. First, complaints echoed among and between the authors and their colleagues without, of course, generating substantive dialogue with detractors.

Next came attempts to dialogue with the media (a fascinating exercise that usually resulted in only snippets of conversation being broadcast, many of which resulted in misquotes and a few of which allowed gems of accurate information about traditional public education to sneak out). Persistent efforts to share data with state legislators often fell on astonishingly deaf ears.

Despite receiving support from local chambers of commerce where many superintendents served as board members and officers, and despite strong support from a small number of state legislators, initiatives undertaken to communicate the value of traditional public education made little impact on a tide of disdain.

Discouragement grew out of the realization that an adversarial relationship with traditional public education existed and that individuals or entities opposed to traditional public education had little interest in either buying into what works within, or fixing what might be broken about, professional practice in traditional public schools.

Instead of collaboration for continuous improvement, the foes of traditional public education were interested primarily in free market theory where the agenda included the destruction of traditional public education, often under the guise of reforming schools, so that mechanisms of schooling and efficiencies for less cost could be achieved.

The goal in this chapter is to stake two claims for the primary purpose of traditional public education. The first claim is that the primary purpose of traditional public education—teaching all students *how to think*—is integral to the fulfillment of the American Dream and US democracy. The second claim is that the primary purpose of traditional public education is required if the nation and its democracy are to erase devastating dichotomies that stand in the way of fulfillment of this dream.

CLAIM #1: DEMOCRACY REQUIRES *HOW TO THINK*

Teachers, paraprofessionals, secretaries, counselors, social workers, custodians, school resource officers, teaching assistants, bus drivers, food service team members, school leaders, and countless classroom volunteers—all public education colleagues are instrumental in the nation's greatest intentional sustained effort to ensure the promises of American democracy. Traditional public educators take responsibility for these public goods that are the greater good sought as a result of educators' pursuit of *how to think*.

When traditional public education colleagues foster this cognitive capacity, the challenges, opportunities, problems, and changes that affect American society can be transformed by successful intelligence, which is the cognitive capacity to make choices that balance individual good and the public good. Throughout this book, the purposive relationship between traditional public education, *how to think*, and democracy is a matter for extended discussion.

How to think is the intentional impact of traditional public education. Quality instruction delivers this impact, which means that "the purpose of education is to develop not only knowledge and skills, but the ability to use one's knowledge and skills effectively" (Sternberg, Reznitskaya, and Jarvin, 2007, p. 144).

Transformative cognitive behaviors (including responsive cognition, cognitive agency, and successful intelligence) are possible because professional practice *leads out* students to the cognitive behaviors that constitute *how to think*. Traditional public school colleagues and students, thus, are in position to advance the baseline of the American Dream: a balance between individual good and the public good.

Constructing democracy means that well-educated builders are necessary if only because (as is the case during any construction project) differences of opinion arise all the time. "Indeed, it is the basic conflicts of values in society that make democracy essential, and it is the ability to discuss these differences in an informed and productive manner that must be a priority" (Westheimer and Kahne, 2003, p. 12).

Traditional public education prioritizes the capacity to discuss differences productively to advance democracy which, by its very nature, thrives when it improves. Improvement is a persistent priority because it can be and must be measured in a way to allow responses to this measurement which, in turn, improves the improvement. The worth of continuous improvement required in democracy is generated by the thinking of "critics who had the courage, vision, strength, and talent to counter injustice, even when the cause of injustice was embedded in the laws, practices, and traditions of a democracy in need of repair" (Westheimer and Kahne, 2003, p. 13).

Continuous improvement is a nonnegotiable in the practice of traditional public education. Traditional public education engages *next citizens*—children and young people—with habits of mind essential to a productive, just, and improving US democracy.

Continuous Improvement and All Students

Great public school districts recognize that all students matter, regardless of where these students come from, what their prior experiences have been, or what the future holds for them. An example of this focus comes out of the largest public school district in Indiana, Fort Wayne Community Schools. Facing the need to update and upgrade school facilities in the mid-2000s, a large referendum was proposed. But the referendum failed.

Where some districts and district leaders would have given up in despair, Dr. Wendy Robinson, the superintendent, began the intense process of redefining who the district was and what the purpose of the district should be. One of the outcomes of this effort—which occurred over time and with significant community input—was a new mission statement that reinvigorated the district. From the board of education to classified staff, and from teachers to school leaders, district staff took to the simple message of commitment embedded in the statement: "We educate all students to high standards."

The new message, the new attitude, was shared widely. Buttons were distributed that read, "All means all." A new vision for an entire school district was born. One principal asked the head custodian in his school what part the custodian played in the vision. The principal's colleague replied, "I educate all students to high standards. When I keep a building clean and safe, I create an environment in which students can be successful."

This level of focus and of improvement is extraordinarily complex. The results of a focus on consistent communication about expectations for equality of excellence shared with school colleagues, parents/caregivers, patrons, and stakeholders are illuminated in the example from Fort Wayne.

Further, the need to engage in quality professional practices in pursuit of *how to think,* alongside the need to engage in dialogue with stakeholders about these practices, is suggested in an observation attributed to Tom Guskey. Rumor has it that after Dr. Guskey talked about test scores with a group of school patrons, he reported that they appeared to be very surprised that half of all students are below average.

CLAIM #2: *HOW TO THINK* CONFRONTS THE DICHOTOMIES OF DEMOCRACY

No apologies are made for assertions in this book that traditional public education plays a crucial role in the evolution of the *best selves* envisioned in a complete enactment of principles of US democracy. The ultimate importance of the complete enactment of principles at the core of US democracy is reflected in John Dewey's insight that "a democracy is more than a form of government; it is primarily a mode of associated living, of conjoint communicated experience" (Dewey, 1916, p. 41). Despite the value of Dewey's statement and the many years that have elapsed since Dewey's observation, it is not possible to claim that a mission-accomplished status exists for realizing balance between individual and public goods through *how to think*.

Nor is it possible to claim that the covenant represented by a balance between individual and public goods is in place throughout America. It becomes necessary, as a result, to take account of the need for and the role of *how to think* as a baseline for cognitively confronting dichotomous elements within the historic progression of US democracy. Four dichotomies inherent within US democracy demand a defense of and support for the primary purpose of traditional public education:

- the well-established concept of the representative foundation (e.g., of the people, by the people, and for the people) of US democracy contrasted with historically desultory voter participation and political malfeasance;
- the factors that short-circuit "justice for all" contrasted with expanding legal structures for equality;
- the continuous growth of student capacity to think contrasted with the nation's struggle to achieve social justice; as well as
- the misdirections spawned by my-side bias thinking contrasted with the brighter and inclusive individual futures that the United States represents to the rest of the world.

These dichotomies symbolize the incomplete nature of US democracy. Also incomplete is the relationship between US democracy and traditional public education because the expression of this relationship can be "conceived of as a dominant narrative rather [than as] solely a moral one" (Fraser-Burgess, 2012, p. 493). Exercising a dominant narrative instead of a moral purpose (Fullan, 2001) deconstructs *how to think* and, thus, obviates the primary purpose of traditional public education in favor of my-bias thinking.

Relying upon or purveying a dominant or majority-centric narrative is the antithesis of *how to think* because, as Fraser-Burgess (2012) observes "the dominant groups can prevail because of their social status rather than because their group beliefs are more warranted" (p. 495). Forsaking this privileged status is the moral purpose realized by *how to think*.

How to think warrants the lived experience of each student. *How to think* warrants a dialectic for public liberty, social justice, and successful citizenship. *How to think* engages higher order cognitive behaviors with the exercise of freedom in US democracy. The moral purpose of traditional public education depends upon function that weaves learning experiences without narrative for *how to think*. The defense of traditional public education is a defense based on narrative-free teaching and learning.

The degree of difficulty inherent in sustaining the moral purpose of professional practice in traditional public education increases if a defense of *how to think* does not occur. Traditional public educators must contend against the primacy of self-interest at the heart of free market theory. Free market adherents eschew teaching and learning necessary to fulfill the promises yet undelivered by US democracy. Free market solutions for the immensely difficult tasks of teaching and learning remind us that it's best to avoid fire-starting fire hydrants.

The Fire-Starting Fire Hydrants

America's fitful improvement of both democracy and an on-again-off-again search for social justice raises concerns about what would happen if privatization replaced traditional public education. Of great concern is that so much of what free market adherents promise is nothing more than context.

Context, the mechanisms, of free market schooling co-opt the language of democracy (e.g., freedom, rights, choice). Free market schooling proponents give mere lip service to the outcomes envisioned in the complete expression of the principles of US democracy. It's as if the proponents of choice schools and the free market are installing new fire hydrants without caring that the "old" fire hydrants work very well and without caring that the "reformed" fire hydrants may not work at all.

For marketeers, reform is undeniably "better" simply because it's reform. But, to extend the analogy, the fire hydrants that privatization advocates install are untested; they are installed alongside traditional fire hydrants without any evidence that the "reformed" fire hydrants function more effectively. Nevertheless, since these new hydrants are a reform, higher quality and effectiveness are invoked simply because the context is new, not because they function better.

While yarns are spun about the value of reform for the sake of reform, proponents wander about waiting to see which, if any, of the new hydrants might work. While the new hydrants are celebrated simply because they are new, the old ones deteriorate from lack of maintenance and a dwindling water supply.

When one of the new fire hydrants fails, proponents blithely note that one revolutionary benefit of reform is that failed new hydrants are abandoned. Equally plausible (when it comes to free market schooling) is that free market advocates can maintain that the failure of a new hydrant doesn't matter.

Of little concern to new hydrant adherents, one way or the other, is that failure of the reformed context, combined with reduction of the water supply for "old" hydrants, puts society in a precarious situation.

While marketeers install choice and privatization as the sure way to put out a mythic educational conflagration, students and our nation are subjected to stealth-schooling that is the teaching and learning equivalent of the Great Chicago Fire.

How to Think *Abandoned by Free Market Schooling*

The extent to which free market schools abandon any pretense of a pursuit of *how to think* is suggested in the use of questionable teaching strategies and lower order thinking learning materials. For instance, the 42 percent of Christian voucher schools that are not affiliated with the Catholic Church primarily use textbooks published by three publishers, Abeka, Bob Jones University Press, and Accelerated Christian Education. Observers relate that these textbooks offer students content and concepts that "often flout widely accepted science and historical fact" (Klein, 2017, p. 3).

For example, *how to think* is jettisoned by the curriculum designed and sold by Accelerated Christian Education. Using materials crafted by this vendor, instruction becomes the cognitive equivalent of "parking" students: "Teachers do not lead students in lessons or discussions. Instead, students spend all day silently sitting through a succession of readings and fill-in-the-blank worksheets" (Klein, 2017, p. 10).

Choice schools are generally exempt from statutes and rules that otherwise hold educators accountable for achievement, academic proficiency, and subject-area standards. Not only is there no state or national entity keeping track of the curricula used in free market schools, but details about these schools suggest that "thousands of kids [are] receiving an extremist and ultraconservative education at the expense of taxpayers" (Klein, 2017, p. 3).

How to think is expressed in the successful intelligence of each student after graduation from traditional public high schools, when each young person enters a trade, joins the military, goes to college, gets a job, and/or pursues further training. When the primary purpose of traditional public education is ignored, however, the endless potential of students in America's schools is consigned to the thought-less, instruction, curriculum, and contexts of the free market.

Thought-Less Free Market Effects

What might be the academic return for students from the varied investments and expressions of stealth-schooling? How many Einsteins and Mozarts are lost in privatization's disdain for *how to think*? How many students' futures are undone by the free market's insidious assumption that everything that is worthwhile can be counted, bought, sold, or manipulated in service to the marketplace agenda?

Back home again in Indiana, figures for 2016–2017 from the Indiana Department of Education shed light on potential answers to these questions via data about the fiscal costs (and the vendor profit) associated with using questionable curriculum products. In the Hoosier State "about 4,240 students received over $16 million in scholarships to attend schools that use the Abeka or Bob Jones curriculum" (Klein, 2017, p. 5).

An accounting of the impact of teaching, learning, and academic achievement associated with free market curriculum materials is notably difficult to find. A moment of thought, on the other hand, about the transformative and widely divergent successful intelligence demonstrated by car mechanics, coders, bassoonists, poets, tree trimmers, lawyers, chefs, pilots, farmers, mimes, dentists, sea captains, and carpenters is all that's needed to confirm that the primary purpose of traditional public education engages the cognitive behavior of all US students.

FIVE

In Defense of Traditional Public Education: Intelligence and Thinking

No apologies are offered for this defense of traditional public education. The primary purpose of traditional public education and the quality instruction that *lead out* student thinking to *how to think* are among the necessities for the bright future that all US students deserve.

MOZARTS AND EINSTEINS

Traditional public education achieves its primary purpose via function that includes quality instruction that equips students with the cognitive wherewithal to fulfill their dreams while contributing to society. This outcome eschews the waste of intelligence, creativity, and individual capability when allegorical *lost Einsteins* (Chetty, Reeves, and Pita, 2018) or *Mozart Assassinated* (Saint-Exupery, 1939) develop out of the adult-centric objectives of free market schooling.

The images shared by Saint-Exupery (1939) and Chetty, Reeves, and Pita (2018) foreshadow what is lost in the implementation of free market schooling. By exalting mechanisms over thinking, creativity, and social justice, free market schooling loses or assassinates the potential of innumerable children and young people. Comprehensive traditional public education, on the other hand, nurtures, initiates, improves, and expands the cognitive behaviors of all students.

But how are traditional public educators to engineer a defense worthy of the futures of all students? Are there characteristics of comprehensive traditional public education that maximize the capabilities of all students? How do educators maximize these characteristics to ensure that traditional public education provides the teaching and learning necessary for each student's success?

A STUDENT-CENTRIC SELF-DEFENSE

The "how" of self-defense originates with the student-centric primary purpose of traditional public education. *How to think* establishes a comprehensive focus on students that depends on quality professional practice in traditional public education. The purpose of this chapter is to illuminate the complexity of this professional practice and stipulate elements of a framework that can be built to craft this practice.

This framework—which is referred to in this book as *function*—is composed of elements essential to quality in professional practice. Function, in the full scope of quality professional practices crafted by traditional public educators, constitutes the "how" of quality professional practice, which is synonymous with self-defense. This overview of the "how" of self-defense starts with an explanation of function.

The "comprehensive" in comprehensive traditional public education involves teaching and learning for the intelligences (Armstrong, 2018; Gardner, 1983) of students. These individual expressions of *how to think* serve students throughout their innumerable life tasks. Colleagues know that traditional public education must include a wide array of subject areas and learning experiences to grow, challenge, and maximize these intelligences to facilitate the application of cognitive behaviors that evince successful intelligence, social justice, and balance.

THINKING ABOUT *HOW TO THINK*

Here comes *that* colleague again to connect professional practice with the theories and concepts that support function in traditional public education. To make the most of the instructional and professional selections that mature *how to think* for all students, *that* colleague would say that, first, it is necessary for educators to understand *intelligence*. *That* colleague would begin by reiterating for fellow educators that intelligence is a concept that invites many different definitions and perspectives.

Being able to speak about intelligence with clarity and insight to inform professional practice allows the development and assessment of lessons that incorporate habits of mind effectively for all students. Selected aspects of the research base about intelligence illustrate practical ways to guide effective instruction for all students.

Fluid and Crystallized Intelligence

This discussion starts with the insight that intelligence is both *fluid* and *crystallized*. *Fluid intelligence* is "the ability to reason, see relationships, think abstractly, and hold information in mind while working on a problem" (Brown, Roediger, and McDaniel, 2014, pp. 146–147). The mental models and procedures that any individual develops out of prior experiences or learning, along with an individual's knowledge about the world, constitute *crystallized intelligence* (Brown, Roediger, and McDaniel, 2014).

Looking at intelligence as being both fluid and crystallized gives educators a way to understand and categorize the mental work intended by lessons. Fluid and crystallized intelligence can constitute formative evaluation of the mental work expressed by students during lessons. Thinking about student intelligence using these two categories creates opportunities to expand upon the capacities students bring into every lesson. Of equal importance, organizing instruction around and communicating during lessons about these two categories gives students models and examples of the fact that their thinking is within their control.

For example, traditional public education colleagues can explain things to students while they keep information in mind for solving a local water-pollution problem that their fluid intelligence is at work on. By the same token, classroom instruction, dialogue, and/or discussion that reveal students' mental models crafted out of prior learning or experience can be identified as crystallized intelligence. Instead of perceiving intelligence as a mystery, students deserve ownership of their lived experience connected with the capabilities derived from learning. Quality instruction establishes that *how to think* is under their control.

Habits of Mind and Three Categories of Thinking

Habits of mind (some colleagues refer to these as *thinking skills*) are the equivalent of the building materials used to construct *how to think* during quality professional practice in traditional public education. Habits of mind are identified by anchor verbs that symbolize the mental work accomplished by using these thinking skills. Quality instruction engages students with the process of adaptation that develops these habits of mind as cognitive behaviors.

Sternberg and Grigorenko (2004) illuminate how habits of mind converge with three categories of thinking: analytical, creative, and practical. Quality instruction makes the most of this convergence. Several examples crafted by Sternberg and Grigorenko (2004) demonstrate how educators can craft quality instruction by weaving together habits of mind and categories of thinking:

- **Analytical:** *Judge* the artistic merits of Roy Lichtenstein's comic-book art, discussing its strengths as well as its weaknesses as fine art. (Art) (p. 276).
- **Creative:** *Discover* the fundamental physical principle that underlies all of the following problems, each of which differs from the others in the "surface structure" of the problem but not in its "deep structure." (Physics) (p. 276).
- **Practical:** *Put into practice* what you have learned from teamwork in football to make a classroom team project succeed. (Athletics) (p. 276).

The anchor verbs in these examples—*discover, judge,* and *put into practice*—connote cognitive behaviors that prompt professional choices of and design for instructional behaviors that engage students in the journey toward *how to think*. Categories of thinking, in this case, give us three instructional frames in which to organize and prioritize habits of mind.

Sternberg and Grigorenko (2004) further illuminate how these categories can organize habits of mind. *Create, judge, compare/contrast, evaluate,* and *critique* are examples of habits of mind organized within analytical thinking (p. 275). *Discover, invent, suppose that,* and *predict* are some of the habits of mind that connote creative thinking (p. 275). Practical thinking can be taught within assignments and instruction that ask students to *put into practice, render practical, apply,* and *implement* (p. 275).

Quality instruction that employs the conjunction of habits of mind and categories of thinking challenges and engages crystallized intelligence when students remember, recall, and apply. Students apply habits of mind as fluid intelligence within this instructional and cognitive intersection when it is filled with authentic learning, simulations, lab experiences, and/or other applied-learning opportunities. Quality instruction creates a cognitive intersection where knowledge and cognitive process are linked as students build their *how to think*.

Function is the framework for quality professional practice within which these categories, and identifying intelligence as crystallized and fluid, become opportunities for educators to operationalize models-of and models-for decision making, instructing, and evaluating during quality instruction.

Thinking about Habits of Mind in Quality Instruction

When educators apply what is understood about intelligence, a foundation is established from which to organize professional practices. Let's return to Sternberg and Grigorenko (2004) and the three categories of thinking: *analytical, creative,* and *practical*. These three categories reinforce attention to student capabilities and create a cognitive grid for organizing and prioritizing habits of mind contained in any specific lesson (see Table 5.1, next page).

Analytical, creative, and practical thinking occur during the interplay of innumerable cognitive "asks," which are the habits of mind associated with each of these three categories of thinking (Sternberg and Grigorenko, 2004). The professional judgment of traditional public educators comes into play when they organize habits of mind within categories of intelligence.

The interplay created during quality instruction between students' intelligence and habits of mind represents the engagement by layers of cognition within the brain to coalesce into what will be referred to in this book as *responsive cognition*. Understanding that student cognition is an admixture of crystallized and fluid intelligence helps educators organize, prioritize, and implement habits of mind within instruction across three categories of thinking to establish responsive cognition.

Not only does instruction framed in this way give students labels to use to think about their own thinking, but it also gives lessons a structure to be referenced in communications from traditional public educators to stakeholders about quality practice. Quality instruction also includes a massive host of teaching strategies like thinking webs and other graphic organizers that put students in a position as learners to mosaic cognitively about the fit among the knowledge, habits of mind, and cognitive process explored in class.

Table 5.1. Thinking, Intelligence, and Habits of Mind

	Analytical Intelligence	Creative Intelligence	Practical Intelligence
Analytical Habits of Mind	Judge, create, compare-contrast, evaluate, critique (S/G)		
	Problem-solving (BRM)		
	Other scholars*—making connections, generate, check, finding patterns among ideas, considering multiple points of view		
Creative Habits of Mind		Discover, invent, suppose that, predict (S/G)	
		Synthesize, apply existing knowledge/habits of mind to new situations (BRM)	
		Other scholars*—activating background or a priori knowledge, plan, produce, imagining alternatives and possibilities	

	Analytical Intelligence	*Creative Intelligence*	*Practical Intelligence*
Practical Habits of Mind			Put into practice, render practical, apply, implement (S/G) Adapt to everyday life (BRM) *Other scholars**—observe, classify, organize, prioritize, recognize, clarifying, question generating

* Other scholars include: Fisher & Frey (2008); Krathwohl (2002); Ritchart & Perkins (2005); Schmoker (2006). Key: S/G = Sternberg & Grigorenko (2004); BRM = Brown, Roediger, & McDaniel (2014).

HOW TO THINK, OUR STUDENTS, AND SUCCESSFUL INTELLIGENCE

The cognitive behaviors of welders, museum curators, lawyers, plumbers, call center employees, scientists, caterers, radiologists, national park employees, painters, police officers, and every other job or thinking pursuit represent the impact of *how to think* in what is referenced throughout this discussion as *cognitive agency*. When educators understand that intelligence is both fluid and crystallized and when they use this understanding to apply habits of mind framed by the trio of thinking categories, colleagues enhance the capacity for quality instruction during which students experience the interplay of cognitive behaviors that *lead out* to responsive cognition and cognitive agency.

The amalgam of responsive cognition and cognitive agency is the evolving application of habits of mind with lived experience that constitutes *successful intelligence*. Successful intelligence is "the use of an integrated set of abilities needed to attain success in life, however an individual defines it, within his or her sociocultural context" (Sternberg and Grigorenko, 2004, p. 274). This connotation of intelligence is the depth of interplay of habits of mind within responsive cognition unique to each student that signals the personal discovery and cognitive empowerment fostered by the purpose of traditional public education.

Traditional public education colleagues recognize that "successfully intelligent people adapt to, shape, and select environments" (Sternberg and Grigorenko, 2004, p. 274). Traditional education colleagues have the responsibility for shaping classroom environments in such a way as to integrate lived experience, capabilities, and habits of mind to bring students into the array of cognitive behaviors and agency that are successful intelligence.

Embedded throughout this book is the understanding that there is no single unitary definition of intelligence. This reality is an everyday opportunity for transformative professional practice within the framework provided by function. Defense of traditional public education incorporates the breadth of professional decision making within function that recognizes foundational cognition capacities in the lived experience, meaning making, and natural thinking of each student.

Traditional public educators across the United States are called to acknowledge the value of *how to think* each time they reflect upon the successful intelligence exemplified by students as they learn and grow. On so many levels, traditional public educators work to engage all students in the development of responsive cognition and cognitive agency. Invariably, traditional public educators are humbled and impressed by the outcomes that emerge for students from years of pursuit of the primary purpose of traditional public education. Students express wisely and well a myriad of professions, tasks, jobs, artistries, and life pursuits that both elude and exceed the successful intelligence of the educators who serve them.

QUALITY INSTRUCTION AND NEW LEARNING

Engaging cognitive behaviors through habits of mind gives students opportunities to build cognitive interplay and takes advantage of the brain's capacity for establishing new connections for new knowledge. This growth is all about student abilities to create mental models crafted by these new connections, which makes possible further new learning about *how to think*.

The talent, creativity, and intellect expressed throughout *how to think* grow as the cognitive capacities of students are nurtured through function in traditional public education. The richness of teaching and learning in the thinking-scapes crafted in each traditional public education classroom are not dependent on the singularity of narrative and lower order cognition embedded in vendor-generated or trademarked activities.

SIX

In Defense of Traditional Public Education: Function

Function in traditional public education is the framework that traditional public educators create to craft and apply the complex of cognitive behaviors within the art and science of quality professional practices chosen and implemented to engage all students in learning *how to think*. Function is the organizing, prioritizing, selecting, implementing, evaluating, and improving of professional practice as practice responds to the learning of all students.

At this point, it's crucial to reconfirm that function *leads out* all students to *how to think* at a cognitive and developmental level necessary and sufficient to choose a balance between individual and public goods.

For just a moment, it's important to return to the art and science of professional practice in traditional public education. By way of illustration, educators know that mosaic artists begin with an end in mind that anticipates the use of resources—materials and practices germane to the end in mind—to fashion a completed work of art.

Traditional public education colleagues do the same thing; they know that the end in mind is *how to think*, and they select from among a vast array of resources and routes—strategies, research, concepts, theories, data, and practices—germane to the learning responses of students to realize this primary purpose. Although this end in mind is clear, the combination of habits of mind and practices chosen to achieve this primary purpose can vary dramatically.

ART, FIRST

Presented with clear glass in a frame and the purpose of creating a forest motif, several mosaic artists in a studio will set to work with gusto. The forest-motif outcome will be realized by each artist. But the cornucopia of different tiles and pieces of colored glass alongside multiple tools to shape them, combined with the cognitive behaviors of each different artist, will result in realization of the goal in dramatically diverse images of forests.

In the same way, traditional public education colleagues strive to reach a primary purpose, and they put a wide range of resources together in very different ways to reach this end in mind. Moreover, both artists and traditional public educators spend lots of time planning and coordinating ideas—lesson plans, sketches, collaboration with colleagues, models, rehearsals—so that the chosen resources and professional behaviors yield quality.

When traditional public educators realize quality in pursuit of the primary purpose, they apply professional resources and take cognitive routes that can differ tremendously from one educator to another. This depiction of the artistry at the core of educational quality occurs to the benefit of all students when *function* in comprehensive traditional public education guides professional practice. Emerging from the ideas shared thus far in this discussion, function in traditional public education frames ideas, concepts, theories, strategies, and cognitive behaviors illustrated in figure 6.1.

THEN, SCIENCE

Science, like art, entails cognitive flexibility-with-discipline. Science, in and of itself, also entails systematic study to understand the nature and worth of actions and structures. Observation, trial and error, experience, controlled experiments—all facilitate systematic study and the results that emerge from it. Traditional public educators must incorporate these aspects of science within professional practice each day to employ function as the guide for quality professional practice.

Function entails science and art in the selection and application of professional behaviors in traditional public education. Function puts traditional public educators in the best possible position to reach the primary purpose for all students. Function (see figure 6.1) is composed of resources—quality instruction, professional assumptions and responsibilities, the end in mind of our primary purpose—and facilitates choosing the best professional routes on behalf of students.

Traditional public education colleagues apply knowledge and cognitive process about thinking and learning to create daily lessons anchored by both curriculum mapping and instructional mapping. Because the resources and routes illuminated by these two versions of mapping are a kaleidoscope of choices, traditional public education colleagues engage all students through the application of what will be referred to as *points of practice*.

FUNCTION IS THE *HOW TO THINK* OF PROFESSIONAL PRACTICE

Function in traditional public education is the amalgam of research-based information and habits of mind that educators employ during *how to think* in professional practice.

Function frames the difficult work of traditional public education professionals when they choose cognitive behaviors that establish student engagement with transformative learning experiences. The actions, the decision making, and the successful intelligence that colleagues employ to this end deliver function. Figure 6.1 illustrates function and the various components incorporated within this heuristic. How these components

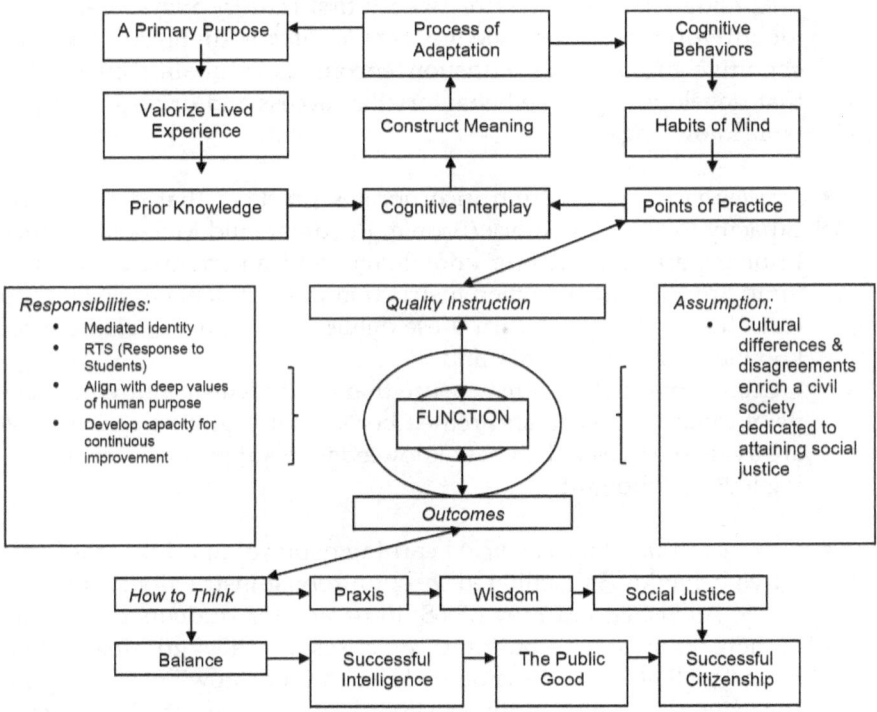

Figure 6.1.

are expressed is a matter of professional practices chosen, prioritized, and implemented within day-to-day teaching and learning.

Function, in this discussion, illustrates how traditional public educators can frame the characteristics necessary for quality comprehensive professional practices. To become both necessary and sufficient for quality teaching and learning, however, function must be incorporated in the professionalism of each traditional public educator and the lived experience of the students served by each of these colleagues. Function is the amalgam of professional practices chosen for students to learn *how to think*. Choices and decisions about the scope of assumptions, responsibilities, quality instruction, and learning outcomes that constitute function establish the professional practice of traditional public education colleagues.

Quality instruction develops responsive cognition and cognitive agency. Quality instruction requires effortful professional cognition aligned with the primary purpose of public education. Quality instruction is the keystone of function. Several studies identify instructional premises whose role in function is nonnegotiable:

- *Develop knowledge:* Detached cognition, thinking devoid of connection to knowledge (Bloom, 1956; Krathwohl 2002), is opinion.

  Although the tendency of twenty-first-century marketeers is to identify opinion as knowledge, *how to think* is divorced from this cognitive masquerade. Function encompasses quality instruction that develops cognitive behaviors that access and/or acquire reputable knowledge.

- *Develop memory:* Function incorporates practices that develop the capacity to access memory (Brown, Roediger, and McDaniel, 2014). Prior experience, existing knowledge, and automatized habits of mind are all available when instruction puts students in position to learn how to bring forward these deliberately "stored" elements of knowledge and habits of mind.

  Quality instruction must ensure that all students acquire the habits of mind that recall and remember so that cognitive connections are available to establish new knowledge in support of ever-maturing levels of thought.

- *Develop learning transparency:* Learning habits of mind that fuel cognitive behaviors is facilitated through robust instructional transparency. As Fisher and Frey (2008) illustrate, for students to latch on to new knowledge—building synapses as they go—instruction must "spell out" the decision making and the "how" of the responsive cognition required for successful intelligence and demonstrated in class by educators.

In terms of instructional modus operandi, learning transparency is created when educators share their thinking out loud during the application of a habit of mind. Demonstration/modeling via the teacher's action/words puts students in line to practice/apply the demonstrated thinking skill on their own (Fisher and Frey, 2008, pp. 22–37).

- *Develop increased learner responsibility:* Student capacity to learn *how to think* cannot be underestimated. This means that as function facilitates professional practice that establishes responsive cognition and cognitive agency, students can develop greater responsibility for the demonstration and application of cognitive behaviors learned throughout the school year.

Learner Responsibility and Successful Intelligence

Creating instruction that employs knowledge and memory as building blocks for nurturing student cognitive process facilitates the expansion of student responsibility for thinking and the new knowledge and learning that emerge from it.

Although some authors (Fischer and Frey, 2008) identify this aspect of function as a release of the teacher's responsibility to the student, function, as it is shared here, frames practice that *increases* students' responsibility for applying cognitive behaviors to discover, create, and express new knowledge. To increase the capacity of students to engage with lessons and to extend their cognitive behaviors further into an amalgam of responsive cognition and cognitive agency, traditional public educators develop responsive instruction and *thinking-scape lessons.*

Responsive Instruction

Sometimes referred to as *guided instruction* (Fisher and Frey, 2008), responsive instruction happens when traditional public educators *lead out* student thinking during lessons and, then respond to this cognition with instructional decisions "mapped" using the knowledge and cognition expressed in student thinking and "mapped" in alignment with function.

Responsive instruction increases student responsibility for learning when it establishes a dialectic between expressions of student learning and during-instruction formative evaluation by the teacher. A synthesis emerges from this intersection of learning and teaching in the instructional responses chosen to move student cognitive behaviors forward.

Thinking-Scape Lessons

Every classroom, every subject area, every grade level can bring responsive instruction alive via lessons that are thinking-scapes. Thinking-scapes are lessons "mapped" so that students apply knowledge, memory, and skills to think into a problem, an unknown, or an authentic dilemma. Thinking-scapes incorporate both collaborative and independent opportunities for authentic engagement with *how to think* (Fisher and Frey, 2008).

Function is facilitated by the wealth of data, research, and model-of/model-for instructional options available to traditional public education colleagues for application in thinking-scape lessons. Continuous improvement of professional practice is the momentum supplied when function is used as the frame that guides professional practice to reach outcomes supported by the responsibilities and assumptions of traditional public educators (see figure 6.1).

A Cautionary Note

Sometimes traditional public educators jump on instructional bandwagons without attending to whether the bandwagon improves or fits the primary purpose and quality. Articulating the nature of, scope of, and successful intelligence framed in function provides traditional public educators with benchmarks with which to judge the extent of congruence of any professional initiative with improvement of practices dedicated to *how to think*.

The skill of balancing sustained practice with improving practice demands thinking continuously about maintaining "what works" in alignment with function in the face of pressures to "chase the new rabbit." Colleagues in traditional public education differentiate between "new rabbits" and models-for instruction that advance student cognition. *How to think* as a traditional public educator means adopted definitions of thinking and learning must be used to evaluate the worth of any element included in the framework that is function.

The resources, concepts, theories, and strategies shared throughout this book, and shared in the learning environments of traditional public education throughout the US, comprise the array of what-could-work, from which "what works" can be evaluated and then applied or rejected as congruence with *how to think* is determined. Colleagues are empowered on the journey toward *how to think* when excellence in professional practice is substantiated decision making aligned with function.

WHAT EDUCATORS SHOULD DO: SHARE HOW FUNCTION CRAFTS STUDENT SUCCESS!

A defense against the efforts of free market proponents and their big dollars can occur with a concerted effort to evaluate how well function serves students. The current and future success of students is what all parents and caregivers expect from teaching and learning in traditional public education.

Demonstrating success across the wide range of thinking-scapes offered in public education permits frequent and clear articulation of the value of the quality instruction and transformative outcomes established through the elements of function. Publishing evidence of student higher order thinking across the broad array of learning opportunities in traditional public education (Strauss, 2013) puts the value and impact of function front and center.

- *List or highlight* the thinking skills demonstrated during concerts or plays in the concert program or sports magazine/brochure handed out to all audience members. Include a comment/quotation from individual students in the performance or game about the value of the skills they demonstrate on stage or on the field of competition. Include a quotation from teachers about the successful intelligence demonstrated by students. For instance, in addition to the usual "appreciation" comments from students in the cast of a school play, include an "appreciation" from the director/teachers that details the cognitive behaviors shared by students.

- *Include, where and when possible, statements* from traditional public educators about the aspects of function that engaged students with the learning shared in their appreciation comments.

  Habits of mind taught throughout grade levels and subject areas should be incorporated in "appreciation" comments from teachers to illustrate the maturation of cognitive behaviors expressed or demonstrated by students. These appreciation comments from colleagues can be included in sports-team brochures, performing arts programs, robotics-team demonstrations, or any other written handout that accompanies student presentations or activities.

- *Share* two- and three-dimensional art projects with the community at local venues, and in the school lobby when concerts and plays are presented on stage. Audience members can walk through the displays of art before the performance and during intermission. Incorporate into the displays written comments from the student artists and their teachers that explain the cognitive behaviors in the creative thinking demonstrated in the students' art.

Or, make a point of posting lists or short paragraphs that share the thinking behaviors demonstrated throughout the art that's displayed. As a part of these "posts," ask attendees to look for demonstration of the listed cognitive/creative behaviors in the art displays.

- *Prior to* concerts, plays, performances, sports events, and other school activities, use volunteers or designated student ambassadors to ask parents and caregivers to share their impressions about the school.

  Ask these incoming audience members about their level of satisfaction and about how school impacts their child(ren). Get permission to use their positive quotes and display them. Give constructive criticisms a public forum, or display how the school or school district is responding to constructive comments for improvement. This kind of interaction—"display" of comments can occur in any number of online or at-school contexts—conveys a broad picture of success.

- *Articulate on relevant websites* how school colleagues see their jobs in relationship to the well-being and success of students developing from function. Share these positive and specific comments from across the spectrum of colleagues in the school or school district. Be sure to rotate the comments frequently so the commitment of all staff to student success is clearly shared.

- *Distribute and display* the comments of former students about how the school or school district helped them succeed. Incorporate specific comments about habits of mind that were acquired at school and that contributed to student success.

  Talk-abouts within instruction that explain habits of mind and how these benefit each student facilitate the development of cognitive agency—the capacity to articulate and apply responsive cognition—which allows students to demonstrate the primary purpose of traditional public education.

  "Speaking" (in any available forum) about the success established when function frames teaching and learning for *how to think* gives parents, caregivers, and community stakeholders a depth of understanding that differentiates traditional public education from the myths, fables, and foibles of privatization.

- *Ensure that active and authentic* learning examples and experiences from classrooms are shared. Illustrating when and how students apply habits of mind during classes allows parents, caregivers, and community the opportunity to understand that traditional public education is a dynamic, future-oriented opportunity for all students.

FUNCTION IS SELF-DEFENSE

Perhaps the most important argument that public education colleagues can make to assert the enduring value of function in traditional public schools is that democracy and the public good cannot survive if the free market of schooling successfully establishes that only certain individuals are allowed the right to learn. The enduring danger of privatization and stealth-schooling is to short-circuit the universal applicability of the public good.

Educators defend function and the meaning of professional practice in traditional public education when they teach the essential outcome of *how to think* in US democracy: individual rights are the right of all individuals. If all learn *how to think*, no one person and no ideology can commandeer rights on behalf of select cohorts in society. Function delivers the framework that puts cognitive behaviors for all individuals in play to facilitate rights for all in our democracy.

Privatization and the free market foster denial of the public good and the destructive myth that inviolability of singularity benefits society. On the contrary, American society prospers when traditional public education engages cognitive interplay with habits of mind in responsive cognition for all students so that multiple outcomes at the core of successful citizenship in our evolving democracy emerge.

Wanton disregard for social justice lies within the primacy of self-interest that suffuses privatization. Traditional public education colleagues must craft function to *lead out* all students to cognitive behaviors and related actions that valorize balance between individual and public goods, as this outcome contributes to the end of the attack generated by those who would destroy traditional public schools and convolute US democracy.

SEVEN
What Happens When Educators Teach *How to Think*?

Anyone who has taught knows that any number of things can happen at any time during any lesson. Some of these are unplanned events: a fire drill, a student throwing up, cell phones ringing, PA announcements interrupting, a cat appearing outside of class on a window ledge. While these and other unexpected classroom events can be fodder for comedians, sitcoms, and a variety of day-to-day reactions, the majority of teaching and learning events are intentional, planned to shape an environment of teaching and learning where students engage with *how to think*.

Lessons in traditional public education, as a result, establish a vast range of intended outcomes including: "aha!" moments in student thinking, clarifying questions from students, engagement in a lesson's topic at a very high level, or even disappointment about having to move on because the lesson was so engaging.

How to think, as the primary purpose and expected outcome of traditional public education classrooms, requires monitoring and adjusting of instructional behaviors to strengthen the acquisition, application, and expression of habits of mind. Function is the framework within which traditional public educators also have opportunities to adjust so that professional practice is sufficiently nimble to account for student responses during teaching and learning.

Chapter 7

WHEN TRADITIONAL PUBLIC EDUCATION COLLEAGUES TEACH: A SKETCH

When the elements of responsive cognition emerge in student thinking, a teacher's response to student learning must encourage and challenge the growth of *how to think*. This kind of approach does not occur by chance but is crafted via instructional mapping in pursuit of the most important outcome for the future of US students.

Within the frame of function, a sketch of quality instruction includes 1) concrete and formal operations, 2) knowledge and cognitive process dimensions, 3) crystallized and fluid intelligence, 4) habits of mind, 5) points of practice, and 6) outcomes including successful intelligence (see Figure 7.1). *How to think* is the capacity to engage cognitively and ethically in choices that balance individual and public goods.

Communicating about Teaching

The vocabulary that speaks to what happens when traditional public educators teach requires differentiation for continuous improvement of quality instruction to sustain the pursuit of *how to think*. Several stipulated concepts (beginning with *points of practice*) are unique to this discussion about the nature of quality instruction in traditional public education.

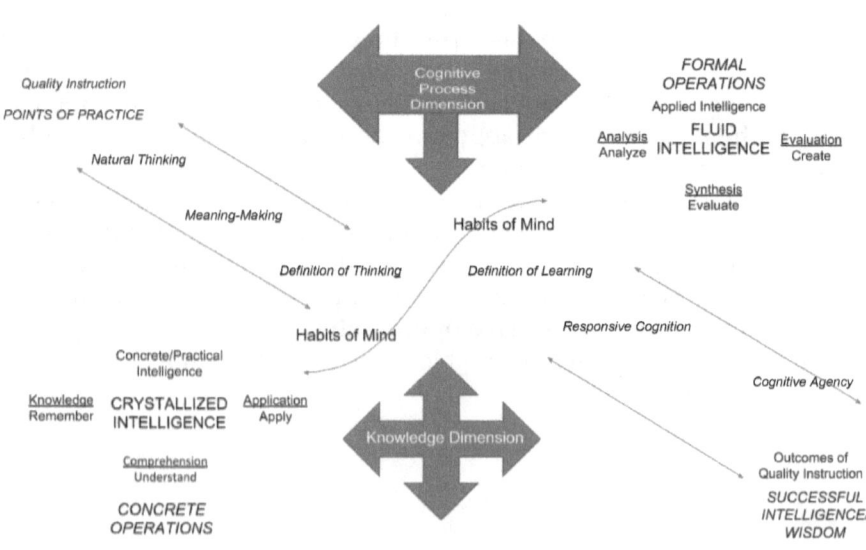

Figure 7.1.

Points of Practice

Points of practice orient the professional choices, decisions, and actions that anchor quality instruction. Habits of mind suffused throughout all points of practice are opportunities to teach concrete and formal operations. Six points of practice—natural thinking, meaning-making, definition of thinking, definition of learning, responsive cognition, cognitive agency (Swensson, Ellis, and Shaffer, in press)—constitute the foundation for quality instruction (see Textbox 7.1).

Points of Practice

Natural Thinking

Human beings naturally classify and organize. Natural thinking is about accessing prior knowledge/experience and gathering knowledge from long-term memory.

Meaning-Making

Meaning-making is a developmental measure of how individuals organize their experiences over time. Kegan (1980) says that "for the human, what *evolving* amounts to is *the evolving of systems of meaning.*"

Definition of Thinking

"Thinking is the systematic transformation of mental representations of knowledge to characterize actual or possible states of the world, often in service of goals" (Holyoke and Morrison, 2005, p. 2).

Adopted Definition of Learning

Learning "is defined holistically as the basic process of human adaptation" (Kolb and Kolb, 2009, p. 42).

We adopt this definition of learning: "acquiring knowledge and skills and having them readily available from memory so you can make sense of future problems and opportunities" (Brown et al., 2014, p. 2).

Responsive Cognition

Responsive cognition is mental work; the cognitive behaviors accessed and expressed in a confluence of knowledge, cognitive process, natural thinking, meaning-making, and habits of mind.

Larson and Angus (2011) identify this mental work as "cognitive tools, including insights, precepts, knowledge, and action schemas."

> *Cognitive Agency*
> Cognitive agency describes the synergy of responsive cognition with overt behavior chosen to balance individual and public goods.
>
> *Purpose of Traditional Public Education*
> The primary purpose of traditional public education is teaching all students how-to-think.
> How-to-think "requires a level of precision and articulation that must be learned" (Richart and Perkins, 2005, p. 776).
> In this book "the purpose of education is to develop not only knowledge and skills but the ability to use one's knowledge and skills effectively."

When educators teach, both knowledge and cognitive-process dimensions suffuse all the teaching and learning interactions crafted within all the points of practice (see figure 7.1). Intelligences are among the primary learning outcomes that develop and improve continuously when lessons engage students in an interplay of points of practice and layers of the brain fueled by learning about habits of mind (Brown, Roediger, and McDaniel, 2014).

The day-to-day nature of this interplay is suggested in the work of scholars who associate habits of mind with intelligence categories. For example, researchers suggest that when creating and delivering lessons that develop "our ability to complete problem-solving tasks such as those typically contained in tests we are engaging the analytical intelligence of our students" (Brown, Roediger, and McDaniel, 2014, p. 150).

Research further suggests that creative intelligence is "our ability to synthesize and apply existing knowledge and skills to deal with new and unusual situations" and the habits of mind captured and explored via quality instruction teach our students to interplay cognitive skills as analytical intelligence (Brown, Roediger, and McDaniel, 2014, p. 150). Finally, practical intelligence involves habits of mind that constitute "our ability to adapt to everyday life" (Brown, Roediger, and McDaniel, 2014, p. 150).

When points of practice orient quality instruction, educators apply the cognitive "how" for intelligences. During this instruction, students acquire, nurture, grow, learn, and practice responsive cognition. When students apply these cognitive behaviors, cognitive agency is established and leads out *how to think* from the classroom into the lives and futures of learners.

WHEN TRADITIONAL PUBLIC EDUCATORS TEACH, STEALTH-SCHOOLING STOPS

When function frames the conditions necessary and sufficient for quality teaching in traditional public education, the effects of stealth-schooling end. Several day-to-day effects of stealth-schooling come to a complete stop when teaching in traditional public education engages students in *how to think*.

Testing Mentality Stops

To take all students on a successful journey to *how to think*, quality instruction sets aside the mentality of *is it going to be on the test*? Professional practice in traditional public education jettisons so-called test-prep practices that are designed to meet the lower order cognitive behaviors emblematic of the age of assessment.

Efficiency Frenzy Stops

The demise of a testing-mentality incorporates the end of the free market frenzy for efficiency supposedly created by rating systems for teachers and schools and allegedly embodied in on-the-cheap schooling.

The Standards Glut Stops

Amid the maze of counterproductive state and federal demands and mandates, traditional public educators prioritize function to ensure that *how to think* becomes the standard outcome for all students. Quality instruction (see figure 7.1) becomes the standard for cognitive decisions reached on behalf of America's students. Moreover, habits of mind become the standard for higher order cognition prompted by pursuit of the primary purpose of traditional public education.

Data-Free Stories Stop

Traditional public educators end data-free attempts to validate free market schooling. When research-based constructs and information are the standard for all communications, traditional public education colleagues provide the best defense against impressions, suppositions, and schooling fairy tales.

Stopping free market schooling in its tracks occurs when research, instructional strategies, and learning experiences put traditional public education students in a cognitive position to apply habits of mind in successful intelligence.

This is why one of the points of practice is adopting definitions of thinking and learning. This is why professional decisions (manifest as quality instruction) embrace an admixture of model-of and model-for instructional activities as the basis for continuous improvement. This is why function—a dialectic between continuous improvement, on the one hand, and research-based best practices, on the other—synthesizes professional practices that lead out to *how to think* for each student.

The Validation of Function

Function in traditional public education forestalls falling into one of the many traps of free market thinking. This trap ensnares proponents of the free market into the mindset that schooling is a low-cost, efficient, least-common-denominator enterprise driven to deliver adult-centric benefits. Marketeers, thus, have little affiliation with deep cognitive behaviors sought through *how to think* and, instead, are enamored of mechanisms and mass-produced, as-brief-as-possible, cheap, standardized assessments.

Function prompts teaching and learning in pursuit of higher order cognitive processes in the revision of Bloom's taxonomy: analyzing, evaluating, and/or creating (Krathwohl, 2002). The myriad habits of mind associated with these outcomes symbolize individual capacity for and expression of responsive cognition. These processes also help orient and guide research to inform choices about lessons and quality instruction. Although it is beyond the scope of this book to explicate the breadth of research that underlies how colleagues can create their own picture of what happens when they teach, the viability of function is manifest as the adaptable evolving framework accessible to all traditional public educators.

WHAT TRADITIONAL PUBLIC EDUCATORS SHOULD DO: PURSUE A PRIMARY PURPOSE WITH FIDELITY

Traditional public educators serve most effectively when they use the theories and research-based strategies that best engage students with the mental work of *how to think*. As an example of how traditional public education colleagues can apply constructs and research, instructional behaviors associated with fluid and crystallized intelligence are suggested below.

These suggestions are not part of a template. These examples do not represent the only way to generate quality instruction in pursuit of *how to think*. Instead, this set of ideas illustrates the importance of educators making informed choices about instruction using points of practice, habits of mind, and data. This combination is the heart of a focus on what's best for students and, as a result, constitutes the heart of an effective defense of traditional public education.

- *Establish the two categories of intelligence* (fluid and crystallized) as capabilities that all students have. Share a way for students to think about their intelligence as prior experience and learning (crystallized intelligence) using analogies or metaphors that highlight the value of memory and "calling up" prior experiences and knowledge when learning something.

  Fluid intelligence can be described with analogies or metaphors that engage students in connecting or linking. Fluid intelligence demonstrated with interlocking building blocks or other toys that feature connections can help young students with concrete representations about their own thinking.

- *Talk with students* about these two important capabilities. Reinforce the notion that *all* students have these capabilities. Share talk-abouts with students regularly during lessons to illustrate how their application of crystalized and/or fluid intelligence fosters higher order thinking about an assignment, problem, group project, learning contract, experiment, or case study.

- *Building a platform* or mnemonic about fluid intelligence can include referencing handheld kaleidoscopes or similar visual referents when students tackle assignments that require compare/contrast, ordering/classifying, or cause/effect.

- *When students paraphrase* the cognition during their application of a habit of mind, educators engage them in the practical aspect, the application aspect, of *how to think*. As teachers do this, they have consistent teaching opportunities to illustrate that thinking is not only difficult work but that working with others on difficult tasks requires compassion, thoughtfulness, and social responsibility.

  No collaborative enterprise, like learning in a traditional public education learning-scape, can be completely successful for all students in the absence of respect. Everything educators do has a direct or indirect effect on the journey toward the primary purpose. This means that a focus on respect and social justice among the members of every class facilitates teaching and learning.

IMPERFECT PRACTICE

In the interest of both accuracy and fairness, this book is written with the understanding that all human enterprises and institutions are imperfect. Traditional public education colleagues make mistakes, and a few colleagues behave badly. Further, this book does not assume that any institution, including traditional public schools, is perfect. This understanding comes with the conviction, however, that all mistakes and all bad behavior must be corrected.

It is necessary to call out bad behavior when it occurs so that appropriate professional and legal consequences are applied. All who serve in traditional public education have the responsibility to meet the highest possible standards of integrity, social justice, morality, respect, and honesty. And educators have the obligation on behalf of students to hold all colleagues to these high standards.

When a colleague behaves badly, various steps must be taken to right the wrong. Moreover, when the processes, procedures, or practices of traditional public educational institutions foster outcomes that do not serve students or the public with social justice, steps must be taken to right the wrong.

Numerous actions that improve, rectify, and/or resolve colleague or institutional wrongs include: owning up to inappropriate behavior, correcting the situation (this must include informing and cooperating with police and other agencies as quickly and as completely as possible), applying job-related sanctions, reflecting on necessary improvement, researching best practices necessary for improvement, putting reflection and research into action, communicating improvements with the school community, and evaluating the effectiveness of change for the better.

The moral obligation of all who serve the public and their children is to behave in an honest, just, respectful, moral, and professional manner so that any deviation from these nonnegotiable expectations will be met with honest, just, respectful, legal, moral, and professional responses that fulfill every educator's responsibility for the safe, compassionate, and empowering engagement of all students with traditional public education.

TEACHER SNAPSHOT: JANET GOODING

One essential strategy we should use in pursuit of the primary purpose of US public education is teaching students how to create a positive learning picture about themselves. As we will see, meaning-making and how to think are enhanced when we affirm each student's view of their own cognitive competence. In Janet Gooding's math classes, each student's capacity for learning was embedded in her day-to-day practice.

Janet Gooding prowled her classroom with an intense, good-natured, energy that exuded confidence. True, Mrs. Gooding had lots of confidence in her abilities—a master of all mathematical expression—but the confidence that she expressed every day was confidence in her students. Her in-class comments and observations emphasized the student's capacity to learn and apply even the most difficult mathematical constructs. Janet Gooding made a point of eradicating what's often known as "math phobia" by encouraging students to take risks as they explained solutions to problems and by establishing the value of perseverance in the face of the challenges inherent in learning.

In fact, Mrs. Gooding made sure that she talked through her own perseverance strategies with students and her perception that errors or mistakes were opportunities to get it right the next time. She embraced an out-loud self-talk about learning. In so doing, she gave life to the famous inventor who celebrated his many failed experiments as "learning about what doesn't work" (Brown, Roediger, and McDaniel, 2014).

Teacher talk-abouts that "speak through" elements of any cognitive behavior are one way to grow student capacity to learn, remember, and apply habits of mind. On the surface, the complexity of this instructional effort, quality instruction in general, and function may cause some to ask, "Why bother?" As Mrs. Gooding's practice personifies, *how to think*, the primary purpose of traditional public education, is an end in mind for all students that is well worth the bother.

EIGHT
How Do Traditional Public Educators Know That Self-Defense Is Necessary?

Long ago, the United States defended itself against attack using the DEW (Distant Early Warning) Line. The DEW Line consisted of radar installations positioned along and near the Arctic Circle to warn the nation about an impending attack. The vagaries of fate held sway back in the day; no DEW Line alarm ever sounded.

Under the present circumstances, however, a warning about a different attack is necessary because the agenda, intents, and actions of free market proponents expose the attack on traditional public education that is already under way. The alarm that sounds throughout this book warns traditional public educators about three characteristics of the free market: the shell game, my-side bias, and thinking-as-rejection.

THE SHELL GAME

Those who would replace traditional public education with free market schooling maintain that efficiency, choice, and reform are a more valuable primary purpose than *how to think*. To reach this purpose, true believers in free market theory run a shell game during which student achievement is placed beneath the shells of efficiency, choice, and reform. A warning is required, however, because the game is rigged.

While marketeers whip the shells around, student achievement disappears through a hole in the table. After the shells stop sliding along the tabletop, it doesn't matter which shell is lifted: strong student achievement is nowhere to be found. This happens because the shells—efficiency, choice, and reform—are both means and ends of the ideology of the free market. Strong student achievement, it turns out, is not the point of privatization and the mechanisms of the free market.

It's time to stop playing games with the futures of US students. The information, data, and theories shared throughout this discussion warn traditional public education colleagues that all students deserve protection against privatization's shell game.

In addition, once educators understand how marketeers play this game, they must act to unmask the deceptive premises behind this contest. The extent to which this shell game is perpetrated on students and families across the United States exposes the free market for schooling for what it is: a profound disservice to the learning potential of all children, the fiscal well-being of families, and the civic health of US democracy.

MY-SIDE BIAS

The perpetually incomplete nature of human thinking indicates why *how to think* is the primary purpose of traditional public education. Without instruction to engage countervailing cognitive behaviors, natural thinking imposes limits on individual worldviews and restricts the possibility of transformative cognition and behavior choices.

The cognitive tunnel vision of natural thinking gravitates toward ideas, interests, or points of view that reflect only an individual's own perspective.

Referred to as *my-side bias*, (Molden and Higgins, 2012) this self-aggrandizing cognition prevents "discernments of truth (Perkins, 1989, 1995)" (Ritchart and Perkins, 2005, pp. 775–776). The good news for the purpose and objectives sought by privatization proponents is that my-side bias, thinking riveted to the validation of self-interest, obviates the need to understand different ideas or different points of view.

My-side bias insulates a thinker and directs the thinker's behavior inward. My-side bias afflicts the ideology of privatization and infects the perspectives of free marketeers. Traditional public educators and their professional practices defend against the mechanisms and outcomes that enable my-side bias when *how to think* is confirmed by data and day-to-day examples from professional practice in traditional public schools.

THINKING-AS-REJECTION

Free market schooling depends upon the natural propensity of human beings "to detect familiar patterns and classify the world [which] can lock us into rigid patterns of action and trap us in the categories we invent (Langer, 1989)" (Ritchart and Perkins, 2005, p. 776).

Validating the outcomes, conclusions, or theories generated by natural, self-originated, thinking proscribes the development of higher order thinking and responsive cognition. As Mezirow (1997) observes, "We have a strong tendency to reject ideas that fail to fit our preconceptions, labeling those ideas as unworthy of consideration—aberrations, nonsense, irrelevant, weird, or mistaken" (p. 5).

Free market theory is this tendency on steroids; privatization is founded upon thinking-as-rejection. Privatization rejects traditional public education as nonsense and *how to think* as superfluous. Rejection of traditional public education allows ideologues to hold forth stealth-schooling as if it is common sense because free market theory is devoted to preserving self-aggrandizing preconceptions.

Circular reasoning like this allows privatization proponents to leap—cognitively speaking—to reject ideas that do not conform with free market preconceptions. Thinking, for privatization adherents, is rejection.

Without an intentional effort to *lead out* cognition into *how to think*, the natural tendency of human beings is to dismiss, or recast, challenges to self-serving thought. Thinking-as-rejection insulates free market proponents in a cocoon of self-interest. Thinking-as-rejection enshrines the limitations of natural thinking as a mental model, which in turn facilitates validation of the self-serving purpose of privatization (Chi and Ohlsson, 2005). These preconceptions permit privatization proponents to think and act in service only to themselves and the limited few others deemed eligible to benefit from free market thinking. The shell game, my-side bias, and thinking-as-rejection introduce the intentions and some of the outcomes of privatization. Woven together by these intentions and outcomes are significant problems, mistakes, and dead ends for learners, communities, and US democracy.

Unraveling this fabric depends on a stout defense generated by the cognitive agency of traditional public education colleagues. The quality professional practices and cognitive behaviors of traditional public educators are elements of self-defense to be mustered to prevent the destruction of traditional public education as a profession. These practices and behaviors in traditional public education defend the relationships between traditional public education and science and art, attachment/covenant, democracy, and balance.

NINE

Don't Say You Weren't Warned! The Dangers of Free Market Schooling

The warning that trouble is at hand for traditional public educators is important. But a warning means little if there's no response to danger. The dangers illustrated in this chapter reinforce the urgency of the call for an end to the counterproductive actions, decisions, and policies that sustain free market schooling in the United States.

The dangers of the free market of schooling are revealed by research, data, theory, and the professional experiences of millions of traditional public educators. The discussion in this chapter identifies ways that the free market fails to meet the needs of students, parents/caregivers, and communities. To establish balance, to sustain continuous improvement in professional practice, and to avoid the inertia of context requires action to negate eight significant dangers within the free market of schooling.

THE ALLURE OF AMORALITY

Lubienski (2013) accurately points out that markets are amoral. The laissez-faire ethics of privatization embrace disunity, exclusion, self-interest, and singularity. But, lacking the courage to balance individual and public good, privatization secrets away its moral ambiguities.

Lacking a moral compass to acknowledge the fundamental importance to US democracy of diversity, collaboration, and equality, privatization proponents manufacture FUD (fear, uncertainty, doubt) (Moyers, 2014) by preying on those whose misgivings, prejudices, insecurities, and/or moral ambivalence attract them to all that's worst about choice schooling.

Lacking the integrity to engage in civil debate about the give-and-take required by US democracy and the necessity for this exchange to advance the cause of social justice, free market adherents seek the ultimate limitation of justice for all via a twisted definition of freedom that is confined to their own self-interest (Lubienski, 2013).

The amorality at the foundation of stealth-schooling is a failure of privatization that, alone, speaks to the value-added qualities of responsive cognition and cognitive agency on behalf of the best of the human condition sought via *how to think*.

The danger of the allure of amorality in the free market lies in its role as a significant roadblock to continuous improvement in, equitable funding for, and the social justice of traditional public education. This dangerous characteristic of the ideology of the free market endows adherents with omniscience, a fallacy of foolishness that, in the long run, may be the greatest danger of all the dangers of privatization.

A WOEBEGONE PURPOSE

Privatization's dangers also include the distance between free market theory and balance. As a case in point, the purpose of the free market is to benefit those who advocate and pay for implementation of this ideology. Privatization proponents are armed with a shopping list of benefits, rights, and privileges accessible through free market mechanisms but only to the relative few positioned and privileged enough to serve their own needs by advocating for this state of affairs.

The failure to create fiscal efficiency, the failure to establish strong student achievement, the failure to benefit the public good, and the failure to valorize democracy, diversity, and social justice are outcomes antithetical to US democracy but that are guaranteed by the addiction to self-interest that taints free market theory.

For marketeers, self-indulgence is purpose enough to justify frauds perpetrated in the name of choice, freedom, and rights. The combination of omniscience and self-serving purpose thrive on and foment imbalance to the detriment of *how to think* and US democracy.

CONTEXTUAL AND FISCAL FRAUD

Advocates of privatization invest in the dangers of contextual fraud and fiscal shenanigans that riddle the implementation of free market schooling. Masquerading as efficiency, fraud is perpetrated on families who believe that privatization mechanisms will not only provide a more efficient kind of schooling but also will pay the full cost of private schooling (Lubienski, Gulosino, and Weitzel, 2009, p. 606).

Fraud is perpetrated on citizens who hear that privatization costs less than traditional public education but who do not get to see the data that indicates otherwise. Fraud is perpetrated on students whose futures are shortchanged by lackluster academic experiences, segregated schooling, luck-of-the-draw enrollment procedures, and for-profit decisions about where to locate and how to operate choice schools.

For students with special needs, parents tend to find out much too late that the school they selected does not have a program that meets the needs of their child, or uses a learning plan that does not meet the standards of the Individuals with Disabilities Education Act (IDEA), or pretends to provide services and, instead, places students in front of a computer for most of the day in lieu of interactive instruction with a human being (McKinney and Shaffer, 2018).

The glorification of context, the mechanisms, by proponents of the free market of schooling is a celebration of empty promises and phantom results; danger develops from the intellectual and societal emptiness that fraud leaves in its wake. Danger develops when unsuspecting individuals are taken in by frauds that are touted as so normal as to be common sense.

The dangers of fraud are systemic to the point that some privatization proponents begin operating a choice school thinking that philanthropic donations from ideologues will supplement per-pupil state dollars, only to find that across-the-board generosity among true believers is a fantasy (Chandler, 2015). More generally, privatization siphons tax dollars away from traditional public education under the guise of greater efficiency while it shortchanges families lured by this siren song.

The abiding danger of fiscal fraud that depletes the wherewithal of traditional public education to enhance the futures of our children is represented in data from across the United States gathered between 2006 and 2013. This data indicates that "there was over that period a 260 percent increase in the number of students who went to school in districts with poverty rates of 40 percent or more" (Strauss, 2015). Gaps, inequities, and shortfalls associated with fraud establish a tremendous danger represented by the abandoned futures of countless US students.

THE CHIMERA OF ACHIEVEMENT

The stealth-schooling fostered in the free market by its mechanisms fails to create learning environments in which students thrive academically. The alleged reforms offered by stealth-schooling fail to establish significantly higher academic proficiency for students compared with traditional public schools.

Studies indicate that almost 40 percent of the nation's charter schools produce achievement results below those of traditional public schools

(Jennings, 2012). For the remaining 60 percent of those enrolled in choice schools, "Test scores for students who attend private schools with vouchers are generally no higher than those for students with similar characteristics who remained in the public school" (Jennings, 2012).

Serving as an example of this danger, a study examining Washington, DC's, federally funded voucher program "found that students who attended a private school through the program performed worse on standardized tests than their public school counterparts who did not use the vouchers" (Green, E. L., 2017). For students and their families, this danger is an achievement chimera that drains the capacities of traditional public education to effect *how to think* for all students.

Free market schooling adherents promote impressions about academic proficiency from privatization without any hope of realizing this result, a chimera as cruel as it is dangerous. Continuous improvement on the teaching and learning journey toward *how to think* for all students through traditional public education is endangered when this achievement chimera is substituted for the real thing.

ELEVATING SEGREGATION TO A SCIENCE

Free market theory abandons the best of the human condition and the moral imperative at the foundation of traditional public education. Instead of these core elements of a successful democracy, the free market ensures that several dangers flourish: stratification, segregation, and self-interest. Stealth-schooling separates by race, by income level, and by educational advantages (Fleming et al., 2013).

Segregation-by-privatization is aided and abetted by the many myths promoted by advocates of the free market. In this amoral market, profit-oriented stealth-schools—some of which begin with the announced intention of serving urban, underprivileged, students—gravitate toward affluent areas where the priority of corporate success is realized because more well-to-do families can pay the tuition and related costs of private schooling (Lubienski, Gulosino, and Weitzel, 2009).

In the same way that grocery stores abandon low-profit urban neighborhoods and create food deserts, marketeers have no compunctions about the learning deserts created when profit seekers flee urban neighborhoods for greener pastures in more affluent areas. Left behind are desiccated traditional public schools where inadequate funding and pro-privatization policies rob students of any chance for equality of learning while giving credence to tall tales about ineptitude in traditional public schools.

The proponents of privatization invite danger when the policy bubble they create ignores Dewey's observation that "a society to which stratification into separate classes would be fatal, must see to it that intellectual opportunities are accessible to all on equable and easy terms" (Dewey, 1916, p. 41). The segregated and stratified outcomes—and intentions—of the free market confirm a troubling aspect of this schooling: responsibility for moral conduct is not a feature galvanized to behaviors in a competitive marketplace.

THE WRONG GUY'S MAD

True believers in privatization and the ideology of the free market do not spare a sense of indignation and revulsion about traditional public education. Since Chubb and Moe (1990) bemoaned the supposed ineptitude of traditional public education perceived in the invidious combination of democratic government and bureaucracy, advocates for privatization have continued to inject their attack on traditional public education with self-righteous anger (Green E. L., 2018b).

The intensity of this indignation blinds the free market faithful to the prodigious numbers of professionals, students, and families nationwide who have made their own choice: to teach and/or learn in traditional public education venues. Privatization fails, moreover, when ideological angst about traditional public education, teacher unions, taxes, and government becomes "counterproductive because it alienated the same overloaded foot soldiers who would ultimately be responsible for turning around poor-performing schools" (Green E., 2018, p. 8).

The time for self-defense and for applying strategies that spotlight the successes of traditional public education is upon us because the wrong guy's mad. The danger in allowing the emotion, the chicanery, and the hyperbole of angry marketeers to manipulate policy, funding, and student futures is that our democracy deserves more than histrionics as the basis for quality teaching and learning.

DISMISSAL OF DEMOCRACY

The dismissal of democracy is another danger of privatization. Free market advocates would have educators and citizens believe that democracy is fundamental to the problem of the alleged ineptitude of traditional public education (Chubb and Moe, 1990; Green, E., 2018).

Privatization fails students and our nation when it dismisses actualization of the best of human beings and denies that the continuous improvement of foundational principles of US democracy is possible or desirable. The dismissal of democracy by free market proponents is made easier when the pursuit of *how to think* is dismissed. Covenant has no value in the free market; democracy's dependence on this sense of *e pluribus unum* is abandoned by marketeers in their rush to achieve what can only be called *e unum unum*.

The danger of the singularity premise of privatization also develops when one considers the governance of choice schools. Rather than the publicly elected school boards that govern traditional public education, choice schools, and particularly the boards that govern charter schools, are "designed to sidestep the unwieldy directives of democratic school governance" (Green, E., 2018, p. 16; Long, 2018).

Board governance in stealth-schooling is exercised by board members whose qualifications for membership often boil down to wealth and the preservation of free market purity. Disassociation between those who govern and those who are governed is a significant danger to US democracy. Free market governing boards exercise power without accountability, regulation, and public oversight (Green, E., 2018). Without the recourse ensconced within the democratic election process, governance of choice schools endangers connectivity and engagement within school communities established by the exercise of representative governance.

Severing this connection in favor of absentee governance, privatization proponents safeguard their priorities: self-interest and profit. The route to the context that realizes these priorities is paved with the manipulation of state statutes. The futures of America's students are endangered because free market theory subverts democracy.

MECHANISMS DO NOT EDUCATE

The free market cannot avoid the complications and contradictions of its mechanisms. Mechanisms mesmerize proponents of privatization to the point that these devices trump student achievement, ignore deep values of human purpose, deny the public good, shortchange social justice, and denigrate democracy. Where traditional public education colleagues seek "the fundamental moral purpose of deep and broad learning (Hargreaves and Fink, 2006, p. 27)" (Leo and Wickenberg, 2013, p. 412), privatization adherents seek legislated context as the fruition of their ideology and the realization of their own fiscal and philosophic well-being.

The clanking sound of the mechanisms that are the context of stealth-schooling is music to the ears of marketeers, but this cacophony is nothing less than a mind-numbing racket drowning out the cognition capable of crafting achievement, social justice, and covenant. Mechanisms are an active danger that delimits the potential of the many in service to the self-interest of the few.

TEN

Mediated Identity in Windows and Mirrors

Absent a focus on *how to think* for the development of successful intelligence, free market schooling proponents prioritize policy and practices divorced from the potential of the lives and futures of US children. The purpose of traditional public education engages all students to learn the breadth and depth of habits of mind necessary and sufficient to realize and express the fullest possible measure of their identity.

The purpose of this chapter is to discuss a question that must be asked if traditional public education colleagues are to live up to a primary purpose and sustain the promises within the capacities and lived experience of all Americans. Before raising this question, it's necessary to return to what is known about meaning-making, human development, and identity.

THE IMPORTANCE OF MEANING-MAKING

To begin with, human beings are always making meaning. From this understanding, *how to think*, as the primary purpose of traditional public education, embraces the vast realm of intelligences and lived experience that all students bring to their meaning-making in the classroom.

Lived experience establishes the value of *how to think* across social/emotional, creative, and analytical intelligences. This range of intelligences is the mesh of meaning-making and cognitive behaviors crafted by the lived experience of each student. The primary purpose of comprehensive traditional public education engages the capacities of all students when function and what will be referenced later as *mediated identity* are galvanized to professional practice.

Educators deploy meaning-making as a resource on a day-to-day basis when they understand that meaning-making is developmental and can be understood as a relationship between the individual and others (Sternberg, Reznitskaya, and Jarvin, 2007). This understanding puts a premium on the valorization of all students. The value of this insight is that meaning-making is about identity.

IDENTITY, AMERICA'S STUDENTS, WINDOWS AND MIRRORS

How people perceive themselves, the meaning-making about self (which is the ultimate statement of adequacy), is shared when "I identify as . . . " is articulated. The universality of, and the universe of variety within, "I identify as . . . " are richly represented in all classrooms.

"I identify as . . . " is an individual's statement that valorizes, focuses, celebrates, and asserts the worth and meaning of the individual. Although it is beyond the scope of this discussion to articulate the full measure of scholarship and commentary about identity, it is essential to articulate several of the constructs relevant to "I identify as . . . " that must be considered in any dialogue about the defense of traditional public education.

In and of itself, "I identify as . . . " constitutes personal and cultural assets that colleagues in traditional public education must understand to maximize learning for each student. The phrase "I identify as . . . " presents educators with windows and mirrors about the lived experience of each student (Michie, 2018).

The impact of professional practices on students also is captured in these two analogies: windows and mirrors. Michie (2018) prods educators into engaging identity as an essential element of function in our professional practice, which is to provide "'windows out into the experience of others as well as mirrors of the student's own reality'" (Michie, 2018).

Traditional public school educators are like windows (via their own experiences and the accumulated knowledge and cognition associated with points of practice that deliver habits of mind, curriculum mapping, and instructional mapping) through which students see to learn and grow into *how to think*. Yet, although windows are necessary, they are not sufficient for student engagement with the primary purpose of traditional public education.

The Windows That Students Share with Us

Students bring their "I identify as . . . " to classrooms as windows that give educators a line of sight into the lived experience of each student. Traditional public educators benefit from this line of sight when it's used to understand many things about "I identify as . . . ," including that this phrase also expresses what scholars refer to as *collective identity* (Ogbu, 2004, p. 3).

Collective identity "refers to people's sense of who they are, their 'we-feeling' or 'belonging'" (Ogbu, 2004, p. 3). Valorization of "I identify as . . . " demands that educators are sensitive to, and professionally responsive to, the realization that "the group identity aspect of personal identity can result in in-group beliefs being more intractable than nongroup beliefs" (Fraser-Burgess, 2012, p. 497). It's critical that majority educators understand that the windows of students of color share lived experience in that "Black students are products of Black history and members of contemporary Black community" (Ogbu, 2004, p. 28).

"I identify as . . . ," collective identity, and meaning-making for students of color involve a host of factors. One of these that majority educators and traditional public schools cannot ignore is referred to as "status problems and minority response to status problems" (Ogbu, 2004, p. 4).

Status Problems

"Status problems are external forces that mark a group of people as a distinct segment from the rest of the population" (Ogbu, 2004, p. 4). Because these forces are long-standing, beyond their control, and laden with the depredations of racism, involuntary minorities in the United States (including students of color) are exposed persistently to "mistreatment regardless of their individual differences in education and ability, in status, physical appearance or place of residence" (Ogbu, 2004, p. 5).

Scholarship, professional discussion, and majority educator concerns often fixate on "opposition" in the response by students of color to status problems. A great deal of attention is paid to the presumption that Black students are reluctant about, or opposed to, school success because getting good grades or doing well academically represent "acting White" (Ogbu, 2004).

Overreacting to this impression, traditional public educators lose credibility and opportunity because research indicates not only that there are "relatively few students who reject good grades because it is 'White'" but also that what Black students "reject that hurt their academic performance are 'White' attitudes and behaviors conducive to making good grades (Ogbu and Simons, 1998)" (Ogbu, 2004, pp. 28–29).

Step Up to Listen and See

Valorizing the lived experience of students of color, forsaking the marginalization that often afflicts the day-to-day of these young people, requires majority educators to step up to listen and see the capability of all students. To step up in this way, majority educators must look through the windows of students of color where reality, research, and respect for lived experience converge. At the same time, majority educators must examine their own windows and how to accomplish the most meaningful mirroring for the "I identify as . . . " of all students.

To maximize the "I identify as . . . " for each student, White educators must recognize that their windows and mirrors present to students as lines of sight into whether or not the student's "I identify as . . . " is valorized. To step up to listen and see, majority educators owe all students professional practices that treat "identity group members equitably with respect to their mutually shared beliefs" (Fraser-Burgess, 2012, p. 480).

Identity as Privilege

"I identify as . . . " is too often unheard and dishonored when privilege is the identity of the listener. As observers of US democracy illustrate (Brooks, 2017), identification, without an ethical anchor of social justice within the public good, evinces my-side bias thinking with profoundly tragic results.

Liberty and justice for all—despite the nobility of these words—is manifest throughout most of US history as privilege. "I identify as . . . " when only articulated as privilege cannot evince balance, valorization, and the actualization of noble language. Slavery, the Trail of Tears, Jim Crow, World War II internment camps, religious and gender discrimination, hate groups—all symbolize rejection and domination of non-majority human beings at the core of historic majority "I identify as . . . " in the United States.

For traditional public education colleagues to engage students with valorization of all expressions of "I identify as . . . ," professional practice must take responsibility for seeking balance between individual and public goods. Thus, function in traditional public education must reveal (through windows) and reflect (in mirrors) for all students that educators value and valorize "I identify as . . . ."

Fraser-Burgess (2012) calls attention to *positive liberty*, which is the "freedom to be ruled by the dictates of one's own reason" (p. 487). Positive liberty, as it is sought through quality windows and mirrors in traditional public education, is the interplay of habits of mind for social justice of an individual's responsive cognition that establishes cognitive agency.

Quality outcomes from function in traditional public education are linked to the understanding that "the dictates of one's own reason shape the exercise of human agency" (Fraser-Burgess, 2012, p. 487). Professional practice in traditional public education meets its moral obligation and purpose when all students are valorized and are aided by learning *how to think* to ensure the exercise of human agency. Fraser-Burgess (2012) adds the vital observation that deliberation is not the primary virtue of education (p. 481). The moral aims of traditional public education, instead, require that all students learn *how to think*, which yields a deeper, more demanding, interplay of cognitive behaviors than mere deliberation.

How to think is the necessary purpose of traditional public education to ensure that students engage with substantive issues, conflicts, authentic problems, and dilemmas that seek solution through engagement. *How to think* is the inverse of deliberation in that deliberation is subject to majority control that limits discourse and its outcomes "in terms of interests and principles that are valuable to them" (Fraser-Burgess, 2012, p. 485). Pursuit of the primary purpose of traditional public education requires majority educators to engage *how to think* as the foundation for a professionally transformative question.

The Question Educators Must Ask

For the good of all students as individuals and for the good of US society, traditional public educators must ask and answer this question: *How do I address and valorize "I identify as . . . "?*

This is not a simple question. Considerable scholarship and controversy surround the statement "I identify as . . . ." There are disagreements and research about the question posed here and the answers that any person might give to this question. Nevertheless, this question ought to be a prevalent part of continuous improvement for colleagues in professional practice because traditional public educators must fulfill their responsibilities to each student on the journey to *how to think*.

The question posed here should not and cannot be avoided if majority educators are to sustain and enhance the impact of function for traditional public education. The imperative to establish a rigorous, high-quality traditional public education imbued with respect for the lived experience of each student has never been greater. To ensure that traditional public educators fulfill the professional, personal, and societal mandate to reach all students, they need to *mediate their identity*.

The Response Educators Must Give

Every human being has an identity. Identity is the most profound expression of meaning-making. The imperative for traditional public education colleagues to incorporate knowledge and responsive cognition about identity into professional practice is ethically nonnegotiable. Across the United States, the windows of the traditional education teaching force offer a primary type of window: a predominantly White and middle class, usually female, teaching force with 82 percent of the US teaching force identifying in these ways (Maxwell, 2014; Toppo and Nichols, 2017).

America's students, on the other hand, increasingly identify across a more diverse range of ethnic, racial, income, family context, gender, religious, and personal realms. As of 2014, the National Center for Education Statistics projected that so-called minority students became the majority of US students (Maxwell, 2014).

US educators come to work needing to determine how best to valorize and mirror because a substantial proportion of traditional public educators have limited identity congruence with the lived experience of their students. Without cognitive agency dedicated to mediation of identity, majority educators are ill equipped to develop awareness about the lived experience, assets, and understandings within the meaning-making and character of many of their students.

Cognitive agency of traditional public educators can be directed toward resolving this absence. The response of traditional public school educators to *How do we address "I identify as . . . "*? should be directed toward creating the best possible mirrors for students. As a result, how traditional public educators address "I identify as . . . " is *mediated identity*. As a result, mediated identity becomes an essential part of professional practice for traditional public educators. Absent a commitment to mediate identity, too many lessons and too many majority educator–student interactions are little better than clueless and often as bad as deficit thinking infected with low expectations for diverse students.

MAJORITY EDUCATOR PERSPECTIVES AND PROFESSIONAL PRACTICE

How the three authors of this book identify extends this discussion about mediated identity. We identify as the "historical privilege of characteristics associated with being White, a primary English speaker, male, heterosexual, Christian Protestant, and middle class" (Juarez, Smith, and Hayes, 2008, p. 21). Wrapped in this identity are educator characteristics: professional experiences, the positive organizational scholarship that influences responsive cognition, and existing service as windows for students.

Family, faith, and education crafted our worldviews. Our parents made it clear that every person merited respect. Church services and Sunday school echoed family beliefs that "love thy neighbor as thy self" and "do unto others as you would have them do unto you" were the expectations for day-to-day behavior.

Our communities fed the stability of the covenants in our lives. And, a battalion of bright and caring teachers throughout our K–12 years in traditional public education gave life to the balance inherent in making a difference for others.

We identify, in a professional sense, as traditional public education colleagues and as teachers in elementary education and secondary social studies. From these perspectives, we acknowledge the role of traditional public educators in citizenship education (Shaver, 1997). Throughout our lengthy careers, engagement with citizenship education springs from an understanding that the potential of justice for all within America's democracy depends on covenant in our democracy.

This perspective takes practical shape from the value of individual good evinced in quality instruction designed to realize the cognitive behaviors that sustain *how to think*. An essential realization about quality in traditional public education is that *how to think* is not about attaining or enforcing a dominant narrative. Rather, as social justice requires, *how to think* is the engagement of the lived experience of each student with habits of mind that foster successful intelligence. In the development of cognitive behaviors capable of choosing a balance between individual and public goods exists the validation of identity, public liberty, and the covenant that are the traditional public education that all US students deserve.

Building awareness of "I identify as . . . " in the lived experience of students does not mean that majority educators can understand completely how students of color experience the world or how much of the world reacts to them. Building awareness, in this regard, is an instance for continuous improvement toward mediated identity. Awareness, for majority K–12 traditional public school educators, demands fulfillment of the profession's moral purpose through mediation of identity within function on behalf of all students.

Awareness fueled by *how to think* demands action by majority educators to be the most complete possible expression of validation of each student. A call to wait for, or delay, awareness means that interactions nurtured by mediation of identity are relegated to the mistake of not engaging with race and poverty forthrightly in traditional public education. Silence instead of expressions and behaviors that validate each student's "I identify as . . . " is an affront to the capacity of traditional public educators and yet more opportunities for students to endure the marginalization embedded in status problems. In the same way that public school educators cannot wait twelve years to engage students with *how to think*, majority educators cannot wait for awareness. Mediated identity is the continuous and intentional awareness sought through the forthright engagement of colleagues of color and majority colleagues about race, poverty, lived experience, and valorization.

Professional Practice for Windows and Mirrors

Educators need to understand that a window-mirror conundrum accompanies majority identity. It's one thing to think about the covenant in the principles of democracy but it's another thing entirely to understand how the personal and individual experience of "I identify as . . . " within our democracy is a devastating, discriminatory, stereotyped denial of meaning-making for many students and their families.

To address the conundrum of privilege and its barriers to valorize "I identify as . . . " begins with majority educators listening to colleagues, students, parents, and communities of color. When majority educators listen to and dialogue with fellow professionals whose lived experience differs from their own, these educators hear that in American education, "the voices of marginalized populations are often absent from the 'mainstream' discourse, and the issues that are most important to these populations are frequently ignored" (Esposito and Swain, 2009, p. 39).

To bring adequacy, equity, respect, and social justice to students, majority educators should reflect upon the wisdom of a Latino teaching colleague who observed that "'kids respond better and connect better to school and their education [when] the teacher in front of them responds to who they are and where they come from'" (Maxwell, 2014).

Mediating identity begins when a colleague realizes that her or his "I identify as . . . " constitutes an unexamined obstacle to the intent and the outcomes sought for all students. Beginning to see from perspectives that are not their own, majority educators realize that their "I identify as . . . " originates in a closed system embedded with disconnection from lived experience not their own. This beginning is a realization that majority educators are effective windows but ineffective mirrors.

Many Windows, Few Mirrors

To restate the opportunity and challenge: How do majority educators ensure that "I identify as . . . " for each student is fulfilled through function when the professional relationship between teachers and students is often an interaction between majority-identity adults and minority-identity students?

On the one hand, educators provide windows for students; quality professional practices allow students to "see" knowledge and cognitive processes on the journey to *how to think*. Students, however, have a limited number of educator-mirrors who reflect "their own lived experiences validated and valued" (Michie, 2018).

Throughout the history of traditional public education in the US, educators have focused on how to be the most effective teachers possible for all students. In light of the continued evolution of US demographics, and in light of the frequent neglect of a valorizing answer, majority educators are duty bound to create the qualities in professional practice that are both window and mirror.

Slow Progress and an Inadequate Answer

Recognition of and respect for the ever-present diversity of students in US classrooms are not constants in the history of traditional public education. Throughout much of the first two hundred years of American history, schools were routinized and/or segregated (racially, economically, socially, and intellectually) to the detriment of all children and young people.

During more recent times, in the absence of adequate funding, traditional public schools too often struggle to find time to discover and invest in research-based best practices. This means that an overabundance of lower level cognition in professional practice results, so that interactions dedicated to social justice within responsive cognition are a priority only when individual educators choose to make them so. Time and opportunity to discover, implement, and evaluate best practices that seek responsive cognition on behalf of "I identify as . . . " are scarce.

Hit-or-miss implementation of quality instruction means that cognitive agency cannot flourish among educators on behalf of students. Mirroring the nation's erratic stutter-step of progress toward liberty and justice for all, majority traditional public educators struggle to establish teaching, learning, interactions, and communications consistent with the highest theoretical aspirations articulated in the theories and documents that undergird US democracy.

Identity and Effective Instruction

Liberty and justice for all is a phrase from the Pledge of Allegiance often accepted as an apt generalization of the American experience. Traditional public education has been long accustomed to including this oath daily as a patriotic responsibility.

More to the point of the responsibility of traditional public education to US democracy is the primary purpose—*how to think*—necessary to successful intelligence and the day-to-day choices that can operationalize liberty and justice for all. Making the most of this foundation, however, requires that traditional public educators heed the meaning-making of students and answer with professional practices that both "window" and "mirror."

Unfortunately, the answer to how best to engage students with professional practices that are both window and mirror has been a long time coming. For the most part, professional practice in traditional public education evidences an incomplete answer; windows and mirrors are not available often enough in the classroom experiences of too many students. Asserting the value of lived experience of all students in traditional public schools is a matter of fits and starts, deferred and delayed by incomplete knowledge of effective instruction, racist/deficit thinking, and/or privilege. Maximizing the quality of professional practices of all educators in all traditional public schools to valorize all students involves a search for adequacy.

Adequacy for all students demands, in large measure, that traditional public education colleagues ask and answer a new question: how does the practice of education most meaningfully supply mirrors for each student's statement of "I identify as . . . "?

REPRISE: Quality Instruction

Quality instruction valorizes the lived experiences of students as individuals develop cognitive behaviors sufficient to thwart marginalization and necessary to contribute meaningfully to the realization of freedom and justice for all. The charge embraced by the foundational elements of US democracy to establish equity is undertaken, in part, via quality instruction that engages all students with habits of mind that fuel responsive cognition for cognitive agency.

Quality instruction is the necessary and sufficient response of traditional public education colleagues that answers the transformative charge given us by state constitutions: reflect valorized, comprehensive, universal, equitable, learning to all students. Unfortunately, professional practice is mostly about windows.

WHY ASK HOW TO ADDRESS "I IDENTIFY AS . . . "?

Questions about addressing "I identify as . . . " must be asked and answered because traditional public educators reach all students if they incorporate in their cognitive agency the worth of perspectives learned from our colleagues, students, and relevant theory in the course of mediating identity.

Asking and discussing these questions, despite being grounded in the best of the human condition, will not align with the current practice of all colleagues. Any unease associated with these questions and this discussion makes this portion of this book all the more important. To create opportunities for a discussion about how to address "I identify as . . . ," understanding the role of windows and mirrors in quality professional practice is a critical step to take.

Cognitive Dissonance, Professional Practice, and Mediated Identity

Serving as traditional public educators means persistent engagement with the lived experience of diverse students, colleagues, and communities. The efforts that the three authors made early in their careers to reach students, colleagues, parents, and other stakeholders who identified in ways different from their own were sometimes meaningful and sometimes complete disasters. Hit or miss, understanding what others brought to the table and what other identities entailed was not a strength they brought to their classrooms and schools.

Moreover, they discovered that school districts and the various rules and procedures utilized by the districts paid little heed to "I identify as . . . " when it came to many aspects of professional practice. For instance, a large urban school district assigned several colleagues as principals to recruit educators at the teacher job fair held by a major university:

> I was the principal at a school with a minority enrollment of 49 percent. African-American students, Hispanic-American students, and students from 17 cultures whose first language was not English were among the children who composed our rich diversity. My mission at the Job Fair was to locate and interview candidates who mirrored my students for open positions at my school.
>
> The dilemma I faced, however, was that our district's application process and various official forms did not permit me to indicate when a candidate's excellence included mirroring of our students. Avoiding any discriminatory practice and complying with state and federal statutes was, of course, the proper thing to do. But, we were unable to articulate our strong interest in mirror candidates and we were prohibited from archiving or noting the mirror-status of any candidate in the information gathered at the Job Fair.
>
> Too often—at this and at other college-sponsored Job Fairs—we had only White and female window-candidates apply for our open teaching positions. We had a lot to learn to live up to what it takes to make a difference for all students.

From Cognitive Dissonance to Mediated Identity

Cognitive dissonance is a powerful force. Every educator knows this. Missed communications, ineffective interactions, and clueless thinking in the mostly windows early careers of the three authors of this book did not come close to satisfying how traditional public educators were supposed to "make a difference." Cognitive dissonance prompted intense reflection.

Based on an understanding of successful intelligence, the intrinsic value of the identities of so many others with whom and for whom the three authors worked ensured that merely intending social justice became little more than adequacy-lite. Disengagement from the lived experience of students and colleagues did not allow any of the three authors to transition from theoretical justice to social justice. Walled off by privilege that the authors did not perceive clearly, "I identify as . . . " was insufficient to the task of realizing the primary purpose for all students via professional practice.

Cognitive Dissonance and a Pursuit of Continuous Improvement

This revelation taught the authors that the full measure of the primary purpose of professional practice comes to naught without finding a way to mediate the identity that majority educators bring to the learning and lives of students. Next steps, therefore, engaged "in the critical self-reflection that may lead to changes in perspective [which] is, in itself, a process that requires self-awareness, planning, skill, support, and discourse with others" (Brown, 2004, p. 85).

The result of this process, the outcome of transformation embedded in critical self-reflection, became a mediation of "I identify as . . . " via exploration of the authors' self-understandings, mental models, and beliefs in order to "look within and honestly confront [our] biases and shortcomings" (Brown, 2004, p. 88). The professionalism and the *how to think* required of majority traditional public educators entails confronting what it takes to be authentic and effective for all identities in our classrooms and school community. Educators need to learn how windows must also reflect.

REPRISE: Beginning with the End in Mind

Successful traditional public educators begin with the end in mind. As the US labors to become a nation that practices social justice for all, the responsibility of traditional public educators to carry social justice into day-to-day teaching and learning in pursuit of *how to think* grows exponentially as an ethical imperative. This means that majority American educators in the twenty-first century need to determine how to reflect and teach social justice.

This end in mind for traditional public education is met with resistance from free market proponents, including state legislators who decry teaching and learning about what is sometimes labeled *cultural competency*. At the same time, legislatures eagerly add one program du jour on top of another to create intrusive, often unfunded, mandates that obscure, obstruct, and obliterate time and energy for mediating identity. Determining how to accomplish this end in mind involves the convergence of several factors: praxis, what's best in the human condition, open-to-learning dialogues, and successful intelligence within professional practice.

KNOWING HOW TO MEDIATE IDENTITY IS AN EDUCATOR'S RESPONSIBILITY

When the authors began teaching, they knew an important part of the job "should be to stimulate people's thinking ability over time in ways which will enable them to use more adequate and complex reasoning patterns to solve moral problems" (Kohlberg and Hersh, 1977, p. 56). Furthermore, it was clear that educators had the responsibility to engage students with cognitive behaviors that provided the wherewithal to confront the unfulfilled equity and adequacy within the experiences of so many citizens of color and in poverty. But these realizations were not sufficient to craft quality instruction and interactions out of limited perspectives and unlimited privilege.

The key to mediating identity while, at the same time, dismantling the unseen wall of privilege that limited the vision of the three authors was found in discourse with others whose "I identify as . . . " was not the authors' worldview. Understanding then mediating identities is a listening and living enterprise suffused with the worldviews of others whose mirrors majority individuals do not hold.

The mediation of identity became an aspect of continuous improvement for professional practice and for the lived experience of the authors. Improving in this way allowed the authors to "window" and build awareness on behalf of all students' experience of family, culture, language, living, working, and growing. Colleagues, parents, students, and stakeholders of color, of linguistic diversity, and of lived experience without privilege taught the authors by exploring, sharing, and confronting identity and race.

For instance, the three authors listened when colleagues shared their life stories. This was a time also to ask questions. The colleagues with whom the authors worked put critical conversations about race into work, interactions, and dialogue. Colleagues, friends, parents/caregivers, students, and community members (including Debbie, Darcy, Maurice, Carl, Eduardo, Leslie, Federa, Joshua, Jamyce, Joe, and Geraldo) invited the authors through their identities into open-to-learning dialogues (Santamaria, 2013). These are also referred to as *learningful* conversations (Brown, 2004, p. 93). The authors spent a great deal of time reflecting upon what they saw through colleagues' windows.

Over coffee, during case conferences, at board of education meetings, on bus duty, amid department and team meetings, while supervising school events, on trips to educational conferences, at social gatherings, and during a host of different learningful conversations, the mediation of the authors' identities developed because colleagues knew what it meant to students of color when they expressed the value of their "I identify as . . . ." In these "I identify as . . . " windows, the authors heard, saw, and learned anger, oppression, discrimination, destitution, fear, marginalization, and violence. The authors saw that what was essential for students of color and students of poverty was "teachers who cared about whether or not their students faced discrimination and racism and [who] wanted to utilize education as a site of liberation" (Esposito and Swain, 2009, p. 39).

Mediation occurred in the cognitive dissonance generated around the narrow scope of the authors' "I identify as . . . ." Although too often marginalized and essentialized in a multitude of ways within their lived experience, the colleagues, friends, parents/caregivers, and students from whom the authors learned sought out learningful conversations. In these conversations, the authors also heard, saw, and experienced meaning-making, responsive cognition, and cognitive agency of identities that resounded with courage, hope, intellect, resilience, creativity, dignity, self-respect, compassion, covenant, successful intelligence, and public good.

Although completely different from the authors' lived experience, the resistance of our colleagues of color to essentialization, alongside their humanity, despite being assaulted by discrimination directed at their "I identify as . . . " (including CLD [cultural linguistic diversity]), brought each author to a self-confrontation with how best to serve all diverse students. The friends, colleagues, and others who windowed their identities knew that students benefited when the best of the human condition engaged majority colleagues to reflect and value identity beyond self.

Mediation of identity is consciously valorizing and validating the meaning and value of the lived experience of fellow humans whose "I identify as . . . " was forged into mirrors that majority educators cannot hold without addressing the difficult questions that too often go unasked and undiscussed in the profession.

TRADITIONAL PUBLIC EDUCATION AND THE AMERICAN DREAM IN MEDIATED IDENTITY

To articulate a foundation for pedagogy that delivers social justice for all students in all classrooms, the mediation of privilege and person that opens the door to the realization of this objective is shaped by an assumption that is carried into this discussion. This assumption is part and parcel of the professional and human characteristics critical to establishing an unambiguous foundation for social justice within the pedagogy of majority American educators.

Mediated Identity and Social Justice

The assumption that guides this portion of this discussion is that social justice is an ideal behavior. This assumption recognizes the complex nature of social justice and acknowledges that numerous scholars have a variety of insights into and conceptualizations about social justice (Reisch, 2002). In terms of the professional practice of majority educators, mediating identity puts social justice into outcomes fueled by function.

Because traditional public educators welcome and teach all US students, mediated identity puts social justice at the forefront of professional practice "in a pluralistic society, [where] cultural difference and disagreement are not threats to a socially just civil society; rather, they enrich and ensure a civil society committed to social justice" (Grant and Gibson, 2013, p. 89). A corollary to this baseline is that citizenship in a democracy entails dedication to cognitive behaviors capable of balance between individual good and the public good. Social justice is a window on the greater good articulated by Nussbaum (2011) where "each person is treated as an end, and none as a mere adjunct or means to the ends of others" (p. 40).

This means that traditional public educators must establish mediated identity so that it is inseparable from their persons and their professional practice because "social justice implies that persons have an obligation to be active and productive participants in the life of society and that *society has a duty to enable them to participate in this way*" (emphasis original) (Reisch, 2002, p. 346). All of America's students deserve the learningful convergence between *how to think*, quality instruction, and social justice that is facilitated by function that is enriched through the in-depth conversations between colleagues about race and lived experiences of colleagues of color. Successful intelligence that fends off marginalization, discrimination, hate, and violence emerges for students whose classroom experiences are crafted by educators dedicated to open-to-learning dialogue.

The impact of teaching and learning riveted to *how to think* and mediated identity is demonstrated countless times daily but never more so than during the 2017–2018 school year. Educators and citizens across the country had lumps in their throats and tears in their eyes reacting to the courage, compassion, social justice, and wisdom displayed by students in the aftermath of the massacre at Marjory Stoneman Douglas High School in 2018. The expressions of humanity in the communications of these students—and in the quality instruction and heroism of their teachers and coaches—exemplified how social justice is embedded within successful intelligence as a result of the pursuit of *how to think*.

The imperative for mediated identity for majority educators—and for all adults when it comes to removing weapons of war from the hands of children and from the streets of the United States—is revealed when students put their windows and mirrors into meaning-making that transforms environments, behaviors, and policymaking.

Praxis, the Tipping Point for Mediated Identity

How can the bulk of US educators, in their identity as majority individuals, continuously improve into mediated identity? The professional experiences connected to function and the primary purpose of traditional public education suggest that *praxis* is a potential tipping point for the mediation of majority identity. Praxis is

> a commitment to extended and repeated conversations that evolve over time into a culture of careful listening and cautious openness to new perspectives, not shared understanding in the sense of consensus but rather deeper and richer understandings of our own biases as well as where our colleagues are coming from on particular issues and how each of us differently constructs those issues. (Brown, 2004, p. 93)

Praxis honors the persistent potential of every human being for growth because each individual is incomplete and unfinished. "Praxis must involve not only study and self-reflection, but also a 'consciousness of our incompleteness' which leads to 'rigorous curiosity' and 'motivates our searching and inquiry' (pp. 127–128)" (Furman, 2012, p. 7). The importance of continuous improvement radiates from this understanding of praxis as the nexus of social justice and successful intelligence.

Praxis is a term of greater significance than "lifelong learning" for the mediated identity in professional practice of majority traditional public education colleagues. Praxis is the concept that scholars reference when they speak to the importance of majority educators reflecting critically on the beliefs and ideas that they take for granted (Villegas, 2007). Human beings who perceive their own persistent incompleteness become open to growth that can blossom from critical self-reflection into mediated identity. "This self-reflection is seen as a way for leaders to identify and come to grips with their prejudices and assumptions arising from their cultural backgrounds" (Furman, 2012, p. 4).

In terms of individual behavior, then, praxis should be seen as a centerpiece of cognitive agency—respect and caring for others embraced as ideal behavior for the public good—steadied by the exercise of mediated identity (Furman, 2012, p. 10).

Obstacles to Mediated Identity and Social Justice

From deficit thinking to asserting technical versus moral leadership; from policies that militate against social justice to denial of racism; and from burdens visited upon educators who espouse social justice to market structures that short-circuit student-centered education (Furman, 2012, p. 5), significant obstacles litter the pathway to mediated identity, praxis, *how to think,* social justice, learningful conversations, and the public good. Studies that reveal pervasive privileging of Whiteness at the core of teacher-education programs and the limited social justice that these programs explore (Juarez, Smith, and Hayes, 2008) highlight the necessity for majority educators to mediate identity.

To take praxis one step further into the realm of US education, to embody praxis as conscientiousness is to be conscious in the world of the myriad impediments that exist for non-majority individuals. This understanding is embedded in the work of numerous educators and scholars who rely on Freire's original conceptualization of praxis as *conscientizacao*, which is "'learning to perceive social, political, and economic contradictions, and to take action against the oppressive elements or reality'" (Furman, 2012, p. 7).

It appears that US educators have two choices when praxis is understood as a persistent incompleteness. Educators can either do nothing to embrace each individual's striving toward completeness, or educators can take action to create conditions for *habitus* (which "offers the only durable form of freedom—that given by the mastery of an art" [Reay, 2004, p. 432]) in US education that forsake silence, eschew essentializing, and abandon instructional pathologies. Doing nothing, however, is too often the default choice of American education when

> through our well-intentioned silence, we send the message that the culture of schools is neutral, that it does not reflect the dominant values of wider society, and that there is no need to attend to cultural differences to enact education that is socially just and academically excellent. (Shields, 2004, p. 119)

A significant obstacle to mediation of identity—majority educators often excuse their denial of the pedagogical significance of "I identify as . . . " with the assumption that students of color do not strive for academic success because they fear "acting White"—deserves to be dismantled. Using this pretext to deny that students of color are capable of journeying successfully to *how to think* is racist at worst and counterproductive for teaching and learning at best.

Assets that students of color possess—the lived experience of a student of color, the group identity of a student of color, and the "comprehensiveness of identity for the group member who trusts the testimony of the group" (Fraser-Burgess, 2012, p. 488)—lie at the core of positive liberty and, in this, illustrate the comprehensiveness of identity for a student of color (Fraser-Burgess, 2012). Comprehensiveness of identity, however, should not be misconstrued as the inability or unwillingness to "be aware of other choices and . . . make them" (p. 488). Mediated identity provides majority educators with the wherewithal to see, valorize, and engage comprehensiveness.

SOCIAL JUSTICE, BALANCE, AND THE PUBLIC GOOD

Social justice is essential to the balance that gives meaning to American democracy. A key element in balance depends on paying direct and persistent attention to the "I identify as . . . " of all students. If no person in a community or society is subject to marginalization, and when every person in a community or society is subject to valorization, then the *greatest good* of social justice gives genuine meaning to the American Dream.

Social justice renders the lived experience of every human as privileged. To activate this greatest good, the quality of student thought necessary and sufficient for cognitive agency that evidences social justice becomes part and parcel of the journey toward *how to think*. Wisdom cannot be realized and praxis is inert amid the natural thinking and the my-side bias that afflict free market schooling.

SOCIAL JUSTICE IS AN EDUCATOR'S RESPONSIBILITY

Traditional public education in US democracy has the responsibility to establish social justice in every learning environment as a pivotal means to improve educational outcomes for all students (Grant and Gibson, 2013, p. 87; Santamaria, 2013, p. 348). Embracing this responsibility aligns with the understanding that "teachers can and should be both educators and advocates who are committed to the democratic ideal and to diminishing existing inequities in school and society by helping to redistribute educational opportunities" (Cochran-Smith et al., 2009, p. 350).

Traditional public education colleagues are both windows and mirrors when they accept this responsibility. Evidence that this responsibility is embraced in professional practice can be assessed across the cognitive behaviors chosen by colleagues and in the outcomes attained by students. This responsibility and the necessity for fulfilling it in traditional public education abide when function and quality instruction are utilized as tools toward this end.

This model-for perspective about mediated identity, aligned with the primary purpose of traditional public education, establishes a redistribution of educational opportunities by taking each colleague into cognitive and practical behaviors crafted by learningful conversations where the human value of social justice is portrayed.

OUR STUDENTS, SOCIAL JUSTICE, AND MEDIATED IDENTITY

Often, the great neglected voice in the discussion about social justice as ideal behavior is that of students. Too often, this is the case when policy-makers and other adults cannot see past the often silly, sometimes dangerous, behaviors of young people (goldfish swallowing in the 1920s, phone-booth stuffing in the 1960s, detergent-pod challenges in the 2010s) to understand the impressive capacities and capabilities of young people.

Our students think deeply, sympathize greatly, and respect honestly. These abilities and perspectives reveal the potential in and impact of traditional public education when windows and mirrors enrich quality instruction for all students. Providing amplitude for thought-filled student voices and providing mirrored validation for students' lived experience should be among the primary objectives of quality instruction in our schools.

This pedagogy acknowledges, addresses, and thwarts the inequities visited upon the lived experience of students of color and students in poverty who are subject to "interracial differences, racial segregation, racial violence, stereotyping, bullying, religious intolerance, gender segregation, unfair treatment, language barriers, cultural clash, drug and alcohol abuse, gangs, and low income" (Lalas, 2007, p. 18). Quality instruction is one essential contribution of traditional public education colleagues to student agency in successful intelligence.

The enduring value of comprehensive traditional public education (where students are immersed in environments where habits of mind, *how to think*, successful intelligence, praxis, social justice, and the full range of learning experiences delivered by a comprehensive set of classes and subject areas thrive) is represented when the mirrors and windows of students demonstrate and reflect aspirations and achievements of worth aligned with each "I identify as . . . . "

These outcomes and the powerful balance between individual and public goods they demonstrate are symbolized in the nationwide school walk-outs of 2018. The first of these (orchestrated by students after the Parkland, Florida, school shooting) originated within, and serve as vindication of, comprehensive traditional public education (Lithwick, 2018). Although traditional public education colleagues nationwide generally embraced this example of cognitive agency at the time, the silence and/or resistance of policymakers to this expression of mirrors and windows illustrates both the necessity for and difficulty of mediating identity. Eroding the effects of free market theory that are riveted to the me-first ethos of free market theory is not a simple task.

Mediated identity is the fulcrum required for majority educators to raise the continuous improvement of professional practice into the realm of responsive cognition and cognitive agency suffused with social justice. This defense of comprehensive traditional public education requires a foundation constructed out of dedication to praxis for mediated identity and dialogue for the public good.

When social justice is an outcome of critical reflection by colleagues who accept the yin and yang of mirror and window, all student lives are valorized and democracy can flourish. When the balance between individual good and the public good is always improving, the demise of my-side bias thinking begins. If majority traditional public educators can bring mediated identity to how they see and what they do in the classroom, the valorization of all students becomes yet another contribution of traditional public education to the American Dream.

ELEVEN

The Context of Free Market Testing Invokes a Culture of Failure

Marketeers value the choosing that is a persistent if unheralded outcome of standardized testing. In the same way that mechanisms are context of free market schooling, standardized testing is a contextual step beyond by digging a sinkhole of choice beneath teaching, learning, and the lives of America's students. These tests manufacture academic performance by the numbers that choose and sort students by socioeconomic status, race, and language. The purpose of this chapter is to discuss standardized testing and its implications for teaching and learning in the United States.

TESTING, ACCOUNTABILITY, AND COMPETITION

A culture of failure—the ultimate expression of the market's propensity for thinking-as-rejection—resides within the empty context of standardized testing. Despite claims that standardized testing constitutes a meaningful measurement of superior academic results created by free market schooling, no significant difference is detected by these measures between the academic proficiency of choice schools and traditional public schools. Standardized testing aids and abets a neglect of purpose and quality instruction throughout America's schools.

Nevertheless, for marketeers, the context of testing is valued as accountability. The results from standardized testing produce numbers that, when grouped by classroom, student cohort, or school, give free market advocates the ability to choose how to quantify quality of schooling. In the marketplace of schooling, testing numbers are the "score," and comparing the scores attained by teachers, schools, and school districts provides an aura of accountability that fuels competition.

The practice of accountability in the free market depends on failure. In the marketplace, schools that do not live up to the scores of other schools are held accountable when families withdraw their children and enroll these students in a school with higher and, supposedly, better scores. Marketplace schools that lose enrollment also lose per-student funding and, based on the survival-of-the-fittest ethos of the free market, fail as a result.

Competition—winning and losing—is the ethos of choice based on standardized testing results. Studies indicate that outstanding standardized testing results are a function of student identification as wealthy, White, English speaking, and non–special education (Popham, 1999). This is the step beyond used by free market schooling to take many students of color and students in poverty out of the free market.

Marketplace proponents assume low-scoring schools will be driven from the free market because the funding derived from enrollment will move to high-scoring schools when parents abandon inefficient schools with low scores. This assumption gives marketeers cover to advocate testing that manufactures competition to sort students by socioeconomic status, race, and language. Standardized testing delivers accountability unique to the winner-take-all school marketplace.

ACCOUNTABILITY ON A DAY-TO-DAY BASIS

Accountability is not the province of the free market alone. When the three authors were students, they enjoyed or endured accountability on a regular basis in the form of spelling tests, math tests, reading tests, social studies tests, and science tests. Dreaded "pop quizzes" meant accountability with no chance to study in advance.

Lost on the authors at the time—but interesting in retrospect—was the fact that music and art classes rarely included regular paper assessments, and physical education typically only assessed students if the school participated in the Presidential Physical Fitness Award program.

Once a year or so, the Iowa Test of Basic Skills was administered. Mysteries proliferated out of this standardized testing experience because students and parents really did not know why their schools took a test created in Iowa which was several hundred miles away. Adding to the mystery, no one knew what to do with the results from this test. In those days, these standardized test results were given to parents many months after the test was completed. Although delivered with a great deal of solemnity, the arrival of the results signaled the end of the process and the end of any meaning for the process.

Teachers were sometimes complimented or questioned about these results, but teachers were not really expected to put the results to any practical, student-centric, use. Results were not shared with school boards, used to evaluate principals or teachers, or examined to determine if changes were needed in curriculum or instruction.

Middle and High School Testing

Meanwhile, as students progressed into middle school and high school, they and the authors discovered that classroom tests were more serious and more intense, often determining whether a student passed or failed a class. Who can forget the massive literature tests that covered every imaginable fragment of *Silas Marner*, *Julius Caesar*, or *To Kill a Mockingbird*? High school also introduced a new term to the collective consciousness: final exams. Who could possibly be expected to remember every piece of the learning experienced over the course of an entire semester? Students learned very quickly that they *were* expected to remember all those things!

High school introduced other tests that students were told were very important to college and career aspirations: The Armed Services Vocational Aptitude Battery (ASVAB), PSAT/NMSQT, SAT, and ACT tests became the gateways from which to pursue future dreams.

Testing to Eliminate the Risk

Free market proponents have a "take" on testing far removed from these examples. To make decisions and to establish imposed choosing as context, marketeers must have access to quantitative information, such as data generated by standardized test scores, that can be portrayed as the quality of the education provided.

Into this belief system during 1983, came *A Nation at Risk: The Imperative for Educational Reform* to initiate much of what is known and experienced decades later in the realm of standardized high-stakes testing. "This Reagan-era report sounded an alarm within public education in the United States, and, even though much of the report's education crisis was found to be manufactured, it had an enduring impact on public education" (Au and Gourd, 2013, p. 14).

The impact of *A Nation at Risk* cannot be underestimated for one primary reason: it was a major report commissioned by the US secretary of education that focused on the perceived failure of the traditional system of American public schools. As a result, all over the country, commissions were created to respond to the crisis: graduation requirements were increased and curriculum and instruction were examined under a very intense microscope.

Under the guise of school improvement demanded in response to the crisis manufactured within *A Nation at Risk*, testing became a reform foisted upon the public to "increase educational efficiency" (Hursh, 2007, p. 498). The report took a cue from one of ALEC's priorities in a strong nod to free market priorities by seeking improved efficiency via a new, relentless focus on standards and standardized testing (Hursh, 2007).

A Free Market Star Is Born

Almost immediately, standardized testing became a star of the movement to create school choice. Claiming that the results of standardized testing proved traditional public schools were inefficient, marketeers used *A Nation at Risk* to signal the arrival of a profound national crisis. Indicting traditional public education for results from tests designed to assess, at best, lower order cognition, free market proponents offered competition between schools and the choosing embedded in this context as a cure.

A true market-based system in which schools compete with one another is preferred by marketeers to the system in which educators and officials from the government made choices about where students attended school. Free market adherents believe competition leads to better schools, and hence better education for all students, closing the achievement gap between students of color and White students (Hursh, 2007, p. 498).

Free Market Logic Blazes a Unique Testing Trail

It is important to realize that testing has always been a part of every level of the K–12 educational experience. The purpose of testing is to allow educators to understand what students learn after being taught. This means that teaching establishes within student learning exactly what is to be tested. This means, also, that tests and assessments are meant to act as barometers that measure the learning of each student. The teacher's job is to assess learning and respond with remediation or enrichment to grow and improve *how to think* for each student.

The logic of the free market about testing, however, blazes a unique and very different trail. Testing creates competition at the core of the free market with the perception that public schools are failing, competition created by choice mechanisms leads to better schooling, testing eliminates schools that do not "make the grade," and students unsuited for privatization schooling are sorted out.

This logic pathway blazed by free market schooling became the route to No Child Left Behind (NCLB). The power of this logic never faded and helped fuel the 2015 reauthorization of the Elementary and Secondary Education Act of 1964, which controlled one of the federal government's largest funding mechanisms for public schools: Title I.

STANDARDS, US EDUCATION, AND THE FREE MARKET

In the years between 1983 and the signing of NCLB in 2002, educators witnessed an unparalleled growth of academic standards for curriculum, instruction, and learning as illustrated in Figure 11.1. In response to the panic generated after *A Nation at Risk*, states across the US attempted to shore up expectations and rigor by applying the assessment mantra "what a student should know and be able to do in core academic areas" (Marzano and Kendall, 1998, p. 1).

But there was a darker, more sinister reason for the increase of standards and the rush of states to jump on the standards bandwagon. By the time the nation arrived at NCLB, an ALEC-aligned group of legislators was convinced that teachers were a major problem in traditional public schools.

Although scholars like Diane Ravitch (2013) observe that there are myriad issues that impact student success in traditional public schools—personal-life crises, divorce of the parents, parents' loss of a job, moving to a new home, being evicted from a current home—the US Department of Education identified in no uncertain terms who was to blame for poor student achievement:

> Teachers . . . have not rigorously enforced standards or accurately assessed students, therefore covering up for their own and their students' failures. Furthermore, test scores are useful to parents because parents will know how well learning is occurring in their child's class. They will know information on how well their child is progressing compared to other children. (USDOE, Office of the Secretary, 2003, quoted in Hursh, 2007, p. 500)

NCLB Spawns a Testing U-Turn

To receive federal funding for education, NCLB required each state to design a plan that addressed the requirements of NCLB. One of the most prominent elements required in each plan was the conducting of annual standardized testing across a range of grade levels and subjects. The standardized test selected by each state had to be approved by the US Department of Education.

As a result, pressure began to mount on states, local districts, schools, school leaders, teachers, and students to do whatever was necessary to meet these requirements. These requirements meant standardized testing in the free market made a U-turn. Traditional public educators responded to two mandates that exemplify the extent of this testing turnaround.

First, teaching and learning standards became prescriptive expectations for courses and/or grade levels in traditional public education. Often, the lists of standards were so long that these requirements exceeded

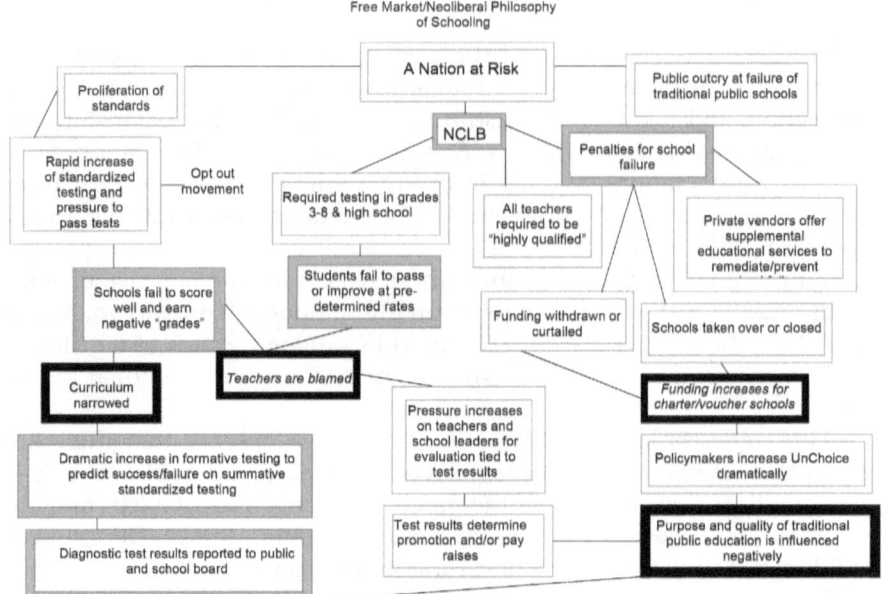

Figure 11.1.

what was possible to teach during a school year. Nevertheless, educators worked long hours to understand the standards by breaking them down or unpacking them to reveal the skills and/or knowledge embedded within. By breaking down each standard, traditional public school educators believed they could determine what to teach to allow students to take the required tests successfully.

The second NCLB requirement contributing to this testing turnaround developed when data was used differently. Although data from standardized tests continued to report individual student academic performance, NCLB required that test data compare cohorts of students, teachers, schools, districts, and even states. The purpose of free market–inspired testing became much more than understanding a student's knowledge for subsequent remediation or enrichment. Standardized testing became the coin of the realm for determining the effectiveness of teachers in terms of covering standards and establishing student mastery of standards. Accountability-made-easy emerges from testing when the market assumes that these assessments and their numbers are synonymous with quality teaching and learning.

While some may question whether it was a purposeful effort on the part of marketeers to require standards that were literally out of reach and to mandate testing to discredit traditional public schools, scholars indicate that these skeptics should reconsider. "The aim of NCLB and other high-stakes testing reforms therefore may be less about improving student learning and closing the achievement gap than it is about undermining public education to introduce a market-based system" (Hursh, 2007, p. 504).

The path taken from the onset of *A Nation at Risk* winds through a time of great blame heaped on public school educators. This path, as illustrated in Figure 11.1, culminates at the point where traditional public educators find ourselves today: battling against mechanisms, efficiency, and choice offered to bamboozle parents and caregivers at the expense of traditional public schools and students.

IMPLICATIONS OF THE CONTEXT OF FREE MARKET TESTING

An engaging concept often explored in middle school science, Newton's third law, states that for every action in nature, there is an equal and opposite reaction. In much the same vein, standardized testing as context has an equal and opposite effect on teaching and learning throughout traditional public education.

Narrowing the Curriculum

One of the fundamental tenets of free market theory is that anything of value being done in schools can and should be tested. Things that are testable through mostly objective means are, then, the things upon which free market advocates assert that teachers should spend the bulk of their time.

> The process of preparing the students for the test reduces the time available for instruction and narrows the curricular topics and methods of instruction. This in turn limits the instructional materials that a teacher can use especially if they are not similar to the standardized testing formats. (Bhattacharyya, Junot, and Clark, 2013, p. 635)

If it is not tested, chances are very good that subjects, ideas, habits of mind, or information will not be taught in today's classrooms.

At the elementary level, the nation's focus on standardized testing imposes instructional exclusivity; writing, reading or literacy, and math monopolize time for teaching and learning. Virtually abandoned are teaching and learning in art, music, physical education, social studies, and science. At the secondary level, "since instruction is based on what is expected on standardized tests, students are not learning real-life skills needed for success in post-secondary institutions and the workplace" (Bhattacharyya, Junot, and Clark, 2013, p. 636).

Student Compartmentalization

Standardized test results from categories or cohorts of students (e.g., socioeconomic status, race and ethnicity, special needs, English learners, gender) are examined to determine the success or failure of schools and school districts.

Students are compartmentalized in cohorts, and educators respond to the aggregation of testing numbers associated with and compared between these cohorts. Individual learning needs, the lived experience of any one student, and/or the necessity that each student can turn to a trusted school adult—all are lost in the conglomeration of numbers and the accountability mandated by standardized testing.

Compartmentalizing students and ignoring individuals affects not only those who may need additional support and/or reteaching. Students who are successful in passing tests are often ignored, especially those considered gifted and talented. In many classrooms, test-proficient student peers are assigned to work with less successful students in an effort to help those students master material for tests. While that may sound like an effective practice, it should be remembered that when high-achieving students spend their school time mentoring less-than-successful students, the ideas involved in the tutoring exchange are those that the higher achievers have already mastered and not material that is new, innovative, or creative.

Other students compartmentalized by standardized testing can be those at the bottom of the achievement and success scale. Students who earn test scores well below the passing line, or cut score—whether they are compartmentalized as special needs students or described as academic failures—often get less instruction than they need because teachers concentrate on a different set of compartmentalized students: those just below the passing line of the test.

"Such educational triage exacerbates educational inequality as the students who either pass or are close to passing the test become valued commodities and those students who need the most help are left to fend for themselves" (Hursh, 2007, p. 507).

Schools and districts spend inordinate amounts of time identifying, compartmentalizing, and working with "bubble kids" (so designated because they are in a delicate "bubble" of test scores just above or just below the *cut score*, the score needed to pass). These students receive significant instructional time either to assure they pass again or to boost those below the line into the zone of test success above the cut score. These students have often been called "low-hanging fruit" because of the seemingly easier process needed to get them to test success (Rindermann and Thompson, 2013).

Testing Pressure Descends upon the Youngest Students

Once NCLB required that all students taking a standardized test (starting in grade three) pass, it followed that teachers of students in grades K, 1, and 2 would be pressured to compartmentalize. Who among the primary-grade students will be or won't be successful test takers?

For many children, as a result, the testing phenomenon begins in their early school career. Head Start children are tested before entry into the four-year-old program. Kindergartners are tested to see if they are ready to begin school. Before entering first grade, students are already on the testing roller coaster (Bhattacharyya, Junot, and Clark, 2013, p. 637). Test-taking skills are taught to students before many of them know how to read.

Teaching in the Age of Assessment

Traditional public education teachers are living through what the authors refer to as *the age of assessment*. What amounts to almost two decades of nationally mandated standardized testing creates a "pass or perish" culture in traditional public education that has changed everything for practicing teachers. According to the National Council of Teachers of English (NCTE), today's teachers are tasked with expectations imposed by the age of assessment including:

- Collecting, organizing, and analyzing data associated with tests
- Grouping and regrouping students according to test performance
- Developing vertical articulation of the curriculum to align with tests
- Coordinating students' assignments, based on test scores, to remedial programs (NCTE, 2014, p.1)

Nichols, Glass, and Berliner (2012) indicate that although the culture of testing has not engaged all cohorts with testing success—a goal mandated for all schools in NCLB—one thing is certain: teachers have become more effective at preparing students to take tests!

TESTING AS MISDIRECTION

The National Assessment of Education Progress (NAEP) scores for 2018 suggest how testing in US education is its own misdirection. Misdirection begins with a noteworthy characteristic of NAEP, the so-called nation's report card—no curriculum is aligned with whatever is assessed by NAEP, and no instruction can be aligned with this test. What students need to know and how they should be prepared cognitively to share their academic proficiency on the NAEP are unknowns.

What is clear is that although the NAEP keeps score, and results from this test are used to proclaim the intellectual capacities or lack thereof of US students at various grade levels in various subjects, few insights emerge from the results of NAEP that educators can use to improve teaching and learning across the US.

Data emerging from NAEP is effective in demonstrating "that No Child Left Behind has neither significantly raised student achievement nor closed racial and economic achievement gaps" (Ressenger, 2018). In fact, pre-NCLB gains in testing on NAEP were greater than the gains achieved after the implementation of NCLB. By comparison, fourth- and eighth-grade reading achievement remained relatively stable over this period, with the exception of small increases for fourth graders (2005–2007) and small decreases for eighth graders (2003–2005) (Nichols, Glass, and Berliner, 2012, p. 23).

Nichols, Glass, and Berliner (2012) found several noteworthy results regarding the "achievement gap" in math for the period of 2000–2009. The gap between White and Black and White and Hispanic students initially decreased fairly quickly from 2000–2003 but then leveled off and continued to decrease, but at a much slower rate from 2003 to 2009.

The Hispanic/Black achievement gap grew larger during this time. In eighth-grade math results from the NAEP, there was a significant increase in the gap between Hispanic and Black students from 2007 to 2009. Eighth-grade reading performance on the NAEP dropped steadily from 2002–2005. Fourth-grade reading initially increased but showed steady decline from 2003–2009.

The hit-and-miss achievement data illuminated by the administration of NAEP should surprise no one. It's completely unclear what knowledge and cognitive process expectations underlie this test and, thus, should be incorporated within the instruction that prepares the thinking of all students since those who are going to take the NAEP are selected at random shortly before the NAEP is administered. Misdirection established by standardized testing is a missed opportunity for teaching and learning in US schools because testing similar to NAEP or AP exams has the potential to restore assessment as a guide to improvement and enhanced cognition.

Politics Test Traditional Public Education

In response to what became the Great Recession, the US Congress allocated $100 billion for education. Most of this total went to teacher salaries, but $5 billion went to a new federal initiative, Race to the Top (RTTT). To be eligible for RTTT monies, states had to agree to adopt enhanced teaching and learning standards (the newly minted Common Core State Standards—CCSS—were recommended). Eligibility also depended on mandating standardized tests based on CCSS, increasing the number of charter schools, and tying teacher evaluations to student test scores (Ravitch, 2014).

Contentious reactions to various characteristics of NCLB delayed congressional reauthorization of this piece of legislation. Finally, NCLB (the No Child Left Behind Act of 2002) was reauthorized and renamed the Every Student Succeeds Act of 2015 (ESSA). The high-stakes standardized testing regime pushed by federal power was ostensibly withdrawn by ESSA. A partial retreat from high-stakes standardized testing in ESSA is a small step in the right direction. However, the modest latitude over assessment afforded to states and locales doesn't end the nation's obsession with standardized testing.

Instead of sustaining free market testing, the strengths of traditional public education ought to be seen as the opportunity to pursue assessment of *how to think*. Avoiding the misdirection of standardized testing also entails a restoration of teaching and learning that fosters habits of curiosity, dialogue, and dissent that are not only the basis for critical and creative thought but are also essential for a democratic society (Saltman, 2016, p. 121).

In addition, while the ESSA appears to give power regarding education back to the states, it still requires annual testing for the same cohorts of students mandated by NCLB. ESSA also continues the requirement that teacher evaluation and training are tied to student test scores (Saltman, 2016). The influence of politics and the influence of funding carrots dangled by the federal government are creatures of free market theory and its manifestations.

Sidecars on the Motorcycle of Standardized Testing

By comparing standardized testing to a poorly constructed motorcycle, it's instructive to realize that alongside testing are multiple malfunctioning sidecars including remedy-selling experts, formative testing, invalid applications, and reward and punishment. For students, educators, and schools, this less than education-worthy combination provides a perilous ride.

Experts Aplenty

Any educator involved in the practice of public education following the full implementation of NCLB can attest to the rapid increase in the number of "experts," "best practices," "school improvement strategies," and remedial programs designed to deliver student success. All anyone has to do is to Google the term "school improvement" to understand the scope of this escalation. An astonishing 29.6 *billion* hits of information related to school improvement emerge from such a search. Some of these cost money, others are different approaches to the manner and presentation of the educational improvement process, but most have one thing in common.

Many of these processes commonly come close to guaranteeing success if and only if a teacher, school, district, or state follow *their program* with fidelity. A more cynical educator may point at the chosen approach and lament that it has not resulted in the guaranteed improvement, but free marketeers usually respond: *had you implemented [insert copyrighted program name here] with fidelity, you would have been successful.* If only it were that simple!

Predicting Success via Increased Use of Formative Tests

When one of the authors was an elementary principal in a large, urban school system, he was approached by the third-grade teaching team with concerns about their "testing calendar" for the new school year. The team pointed out that over the course of the entire coming school year, there was only one week in which there was no form of formative or summative assessment. The team asked without any animosity, trepidation, or hesitancy, "if we are spending this much time testing, when exactly are we going to teach?" Unfortunately, the only possible answer is that the age of assessment has a life of its own.

THE SAGA OF REWARD AND PUNISHMENT: THE MEANING OF TEST RESULTS

Why are tests given in school, and what do test results mean? In the most direct sense, a teacher's test is designed and given to figure out what a student knows after a topic has been taught. Assuming the topic builds on previous topics and sets the stage for upcoming topics, test results are used to determine whether to remediate or enrich what each student learned.

Across the nation, teachers imperfectly test with this paradigm as their template. Across the nation, standardized testing turns this template upside down. Standardized testing becomes a matter of reward and punishment.

Turning Lemonade into a Lemon: A Case Study

One of the authors of this book was trained, as an elementary principal, in the use of a very popular online diagnostic test for students. Results from this test were intended to guide educators to select and implement data-driven instruction for students.

Administered periodically during the school year, this test was composed of questions with varied difficulty levels to gauge the knowledge of students in the most accurate way possible. Teachers were given exceptional professional development about not only the administration of the test but also about how to use the results to help students improve.

Students seemed to enjoy the test, and the school created a very simple but effective recognition process to encourage students to attempt their personal best. At the end of each day of testing, two lists were given to the office: students who had "hit the mark" (benchmarks established for their grade levels) and those who showed improvement (even if it were only one point higher than the last time they took the test).

Student names were read over the school intercom system during each day of the testing window, and they were invited to the office to receive an incentive folder labeled either "I Hit the Mark" or "I Improved." Teachers and students from grade-level classrooms uninvolved in the testing lined the hallways to cheer students on the way to collect their folders. Students kept and used the folders until they literally fell apart from wear and tear.

Students who were not successful in either area (achieving the cut score or showing even a point of improvement) were constantly encouraged and supported with specific ways to think the next time. Because one of the categories was showing improvement of a single point, almost every student earned a folder and recognition.

Great approach, right? But then, the worst possible thing happened. An over-ambitious first-time superintendent decided that the scores should be used to show the board of school trustees that although some teachers, grades, and schools and the district overall performed well, other segments of the district performed poorly. A test designed to assist teachers by providing data that allowed a focus on improving instruction became yet one more way to shame and target unsuccessful teachers and schools.

Performance Incentives and Penalties

The results from standardized testing required by NCLB were used to calculate Adequate Yearly Progress, or AYP. Adequate Yearly Progress was the tightly enforced requirement that schools, districts, and states demonstrate testing success for all student cohorts each year. To "make AYP," to achieve standardized testing success, meant reaching stipulated levels of ever-increasing percentages of students passing the test in each cohort, student learning growth since the prior year, student attendance, and graduation rates.

Either failing to "make AYP," or "making AYP," led to sanctions against or for schools. Making AYP could bring rewards to teachers (bonuses) and schools (positive reviews in local newspapers), whereas failure could bring severe penalties to teachers and principals (termination), to schools (closure or "take-over"), and to students (denied diploma or retained in grade) (Nichols, Glass, and Berliner, 2012, p. 3).

Keeping Score

Keeping score using standardized testing continues to be the name of the game, even though NCLB and AYP have been phased out. Putting students in position to improve and grow their learning based on the results of standardized tests continues to be an afterthought—tests given in spring do not generate data until the next fall—because data from these tests does not segue with grade levels, standards, or teachers that were in place when students took the test.

Looking backward when standardized test results arrive, teachers attempt to mesh old and new standards while moving forward in the learning life of all students. When test results are used to keep score and penalize schools and educators, students lose.

Standards, Get Your Fresh, Hot, Delicious Standards Here!

At any sports venue, vendors hawk concessions as they prowl the aisles. They "advertise" their products with shouts about fresh, hot, or delicious items. For traditional public educators, academic standards are like concessions at the ball park: they are countless, they are all different, and they change every time a new shout goes up about fresh, hot, delicious standards of learning.

Who's on First: The Standards Comedy Routine

Moving targets are impossible to hit. Like the epic baseball-infused comedy routine, "Who's on First?" (Abbott & Costello), standards for teaching and learning are a moving, confusing, and aggravating tumult of targets. And, these are the targets supposedly embedded within standardized tests.

Like many other states, Indiana has seen its share of changes to the standards that must be taught by teachers and mastered by students. For traditional public educators who are committed to meeting expectations and guiding students to success, the standards concession stand is a confusing welter of conceptual, definitional, and procedural options. As an example, for many years, the State of Indiana wrote, edited, and re-edited what were known as the Indiana Academic Standards. These were supposed to be the final word about what students should know and be able to do. But they were written, edited, rewritten, and edited again while teachers tried to keep up and while students took tests based on the most recent standards that did not align with what had been taught.

While educators and students attempted to adapt to this kaleidoscope of swirling standards, politics at the national level altered Indiana's standards palette dramatically. In an effort to garner RTTT funding, Indiana's superintendent of public instruction convinced the state legislature to adopt the Common Core State Standards instead of the homegrown standards.

Any machinery influenced by politics contains lots of moving parts, and the standards machine in education is no different. A timetable was established to begin the process of switching over from Indiana Academic Standards to Common Core State Standards, adopted by the Council of Chief State School Officers. Meanwhile, ALEC opposed the adoption of Common Core State Standards in December 2011 with its model bill, Comprehensive Legislative Package Opposing the Common Core State Standards Initiative.

However, ALEC reversed its position and became a strong supporter of CCSS. Shortly thereafter, Wireless Generation—a tech company member of ALEC—secured a contract from New York City Public Schools worth $12.5 million to create a CCSS assessment for the district (Schneider, 2013). In Indiana, partway through the CCSS implementation process, the Tea Party emerged in the Hoosier State. Subsequently, a decision was made to pull Indiana out of the collection of states that had signed on to CCSS.

Detractors of the Common Core State Standards often stated that Indiana already had "world-class academic standards." So, with support from the General Assembly, Indiana switched testing gears yet again and adopted what were called Indiana's College and Career Ready Academic Standards (aka "Common Core Lite"). These, for all practical purposes, look and sound like Common Core State Standards.

While legislators and politicians jumped from standards to standards, teachers and students paid the price. Across the state, literally thousands of teachers rewrote and reworked curriculum materials, first to align with Indiana Academic Standards, then with CCSS, and then finally with Indiana College and Career Ready Academic Standards. The mantra "what students need to know and be able to do" became a pinball careening through teaching and learning across Indiana because of standardized testing. Moreover, so topsy-turvy were Indiana's standards and the standardized testing attached to them that keeping score by attaching letter grades to schools and school districts became impossible.

Standardized Testing: A Technological Pinball Machine

From the perspective of educators, Indiana's tortured testing journey—first Indiana Academic Standards, then early adopters of Common Core State Standards (with initial implementation), then a rejection of Common Core and the adoption of Indiana College and Career Ready

Academic Standards—felt like traveling through a pinball machine. Battered by constantly changing standards, Indiana's teachers and assessments bounced off three different test providers: from McGraw-Hill to Pearson to American Institutes for Research testing. As standards changed and test vendors came and went, Indiana's testing pinball machine went high tech. Formerly conducted using "pencil and paper," standardized testing in Indiana transitioned to online implementation.

Online standardized testing was adopted to save money and to speed up the time it took to score and return these tests. But online testing subjected students to technology failures; computer-driven tests stalled and/or shut down completely. Imagine the growing confusion, the increasing panic, the decreasing focus and declining morale of students when, after working hard all year and getting excited and pumped up by do-your-best-on-the-test rallies, they found that instead of being able to answer one question then another, all they experienced was a spinning hourglass on the testing computer's screen for up to twenty minutes at a time.

Imagine the frustration level of teachers who spent all year targeting instruction to cover the standards espoused by the State of Indiana only to find out that student success on the test depended not so much on learning as on the online testing platform that mangled student input. Even after the initial years of persistent platform malfunctions, online administration of standardized testing in the Hoosier State continued to feature computer glitches and test-question snafus.

DEFENDING TRADITIONAL PUBLIC EDUCATION THROUGH ASSESSMENT

The primary purpose of traditional public education, and really all education for that matter, is to prepare students for life by teaching them how to engage in the process of thinking. But standardized testing constitutes assessment that replaces *how to think* with rote memorization and test-prep learning. Sternberg (2017) depicts this misdirection in that "becoming an expert in the skills required for taking multiple-choice tests may crowd out the skills needed for other life challenges—namely, those required for creative and wise thinking" (p. 69). A key to the defense of traditional public education, then, is the rejection of testing that necessitates the abandonment of *how to think* while it stymies the continuous improvement required to make the most of the futures of all students.

Sternberg (2017) provides a useful distinction between testing *how to think* (divergent) and testing lower order cognition (convergent). Standardized testing is convergent; looking for a right answer. Such assessment implies that students have been taught, and memorized, the one "correct" answer. Testing *how to think* is divergent. Not only do many possible answers exist when students are taught *how to think*, but there are myriad ways to locate, research, debate, phrase, or calculate a given answer. Divergent assessment tests students' interplay of knowledge and cognitive process across layers of cognitive behaviors. Such tests engage the habits of mind learned by a student to establish responsive cognition that supports cognitive agency and successful intelligence.

Why is it important for students to move cognitively beyond the canned recitation of oft-repeated facts to the level of *how to think*? Sternberg (2017) gives three reasons:

> First, in everyday life, creativity is at least as important as, and arguably more important than, general intelligence....
> Second, one might argue that in today's world, wisdom exceeds both creativity and intelligence in importance....
> Finally, solving the problems in our homes, communities, nation, and world requires more than intelligence. It requires a balance of creativity, intelligence, and wisdom: creativity to generate new ideas, intelligence to vet the quality of the ideas, and wisdom to ensure that the ideas serve a common good. (p. 71)

In these three reasons lie additional means by which traditional public educators can defend professional practice. Assessment as self-defense in traditional public education carries with it the full measure of purpose and quality that students have experienced in the classroom.

HAS THE CONTEXT OF TESTING CREATED A CULTURE OF FAILURE?

Many voices clamor for attention on the topic of testing, and whole movements express opposition to the seeming fascination in the US with standardized testing. Gerald W. Bracey (2009), a longtime critic of the "crisis" appellation ascribed to traditional public schools, said that if testing showed up later in life as important to life itself or to the economy, it could potentially be important as an essential element in traditional public education. However, as he states wisely, "No research shows anything other than test scores predict grades and other test scores" (p. 105).

Tests that have the potential to assess *how to think* illuminate the other side of the assessment coin. Ravitch (2013) reports that NAEP scores show that students actually are performing better than they did in the 1970s and even the 1990s. She concludes, "Let's recognize the progress that our educators and students have made, give credit where credit is due, and offer educators the encouragement and support to continue their important work" (p. 54). Overall, as Ravitch (2013) notes, while there is a steady stream of voices that argue that America's schools are a lost cause and are in a hopeless trend toward abject failure, this simply is not the truth.

The headlong quest for answers to the challenges in education today through the relentless imposition of standardized testing has accomplished one very damaging thing: there is now a perception that traditional public education and its teachers are not to be valued and that privatization is the only answer to "save American education." The damage is done when the context that is standardized testing has nothing to do with better teaching and learning but everything to do with the choice made by free market proponents to walk away from students, quality instruction, and function.

WHERE DO TRADITIONAL PUBLIC EDUCATORS GO FROM HERE?

There are many answers to the question of "where do we go from here?" during a consideration of the misguided, headlong, pursuit of testing perfection. Even if traditional public educators had a magic lamp and asked the genie to make standardized testing simply go away, it's unlikely that the negative effects would also disappear. The lingering teaching and learning disasters inherent in the free market, its mechanisms, and standardized tests reveal that what has been given up in this "age of assessment" is not worth what it has cost. Overinvestment in testing levies a tremendous cost on students, teachers, schools, districts, and states in the presumption that the only things in teaching and learning that are important are things that can be assessed via a standardized test.

WHAT EDUCATORS SHOULD DO: CHOOSE TO IGNORE STANDARDIZED TESTING

For the time being, traditional public educators must assume that standardized testing is not going away. Even if determined parents decide to "opt out" of standardized testing, legislatures and state departments of education will wait to determine the political cost of retaining these tests.

With this in mind, the defense of traditional public education can be advanced by taking several important actions:

1. *Move away* from one test determining the success or failure of a student, a teacher, a school, a district, or even a state. There is no way that one test, even if it stretches over several days, can capture the essence of what students have learned and are able to do over the course of a school year if *how to think* is the primary purpose.
2. *Stop using* summative test scores to determine a teacher's success in the classroom and equating test numbers with compensation of any kind, including bonuses.

3. *Begin communicating* about the need to fund traditional public education properly. Proper funding across all communities destroys the alleged need for bonuses tied to test results. Teachers do not work harder or faster for meager bonuses; they deal in the dreams and aspirations of our nation's greatest resource—students—and should not have to protest to receive proper compensation.
4. *Stop eliminating* subjects that do not fit well into a testing mantra. Even Albert Einstein was reported to have said that not everything that counts can be counted and not everything that can be counted, counts. For many students, art, music, and physical education are the classes in which they are most successful, and success breeds success.
5. *Don't allow* vendor monopolies. It's time to de-couple policymaking decisions that permit the same company to create both the curricular materials for schools and the standardized test that defines the success or failure of students, teachers, schools, and districts.
6. *Ensure the purchase* of testing technology that works flawlessly, or stop wasting time and money on technology-based testing. It is not fair to anyone when the test platform may be responsible for more failures than any other factor.
7. *Know* what is being testing. Common Core or state-based standards are not what determine success or failure. If it's important to keep testing summatively, it is only fair to teachers and students that the standards upon which testing is based are shared well in advance and that these standards do not change without adequate time for teaching and learning.

Has the context of testing created a culture of failure? Teachers and administrators give their best efforts, their most deeply applied wisdom, and literally their very lives to the transformative teaching and learning known as *traditional public education*. Rather than gin up a façade that leads to failure when tests do not measure the higher order learning that students deserve, it is time to implement assessment for *how to think*. Standardized tests as they have existed do not meaningfully represent educators, students, or traditional public schools.

TWELVE

Tales, Stories, Fables, and Myths in the Free Market

Defending traditional public education occurs when quality instruction is crafted and shared. But defense also necessitates calling out the myths and fables that are used to denigrate traditional public education. Free market proponents are avid storytellers. Tales, stories, and fables help to cajole the public into accepting that the characteristics of choice education are benign.

The optimism and omniscience woven into free market storytelling sets the stage for the great myths of free market schooling. Like most myths, the grandiose epics of privatization establish a villain (traditional public education) whose unsavory ways are undone by a remarkable hero (free markets and choice education). And, just like other myths, the stories concocted by the opponents of traditional public education are based on fantasy, half-truth, and my-side bias.

Of greater consequence to the primary purpose of traditional public education, these fables embody a dissociated perspective about teaching and learning. Vouchers, charter schools, and tax credits are among the super powers given to privatization's remarkable hero and the happiest ending envisioned in the myths of privatization is stealth-schooling. Tall tales about stealth-schooling deliver the tenets of free market theory (efficiency, less government, reform) in the guise of multiple advantages for students. Stealth-schooling is the pretense that cloaks the agenda, mechanisms, tenets, and outcomes sought in a free market.

Stealth-schooling foists mechanisms and the rampant pecuniary self-interest of privatization on unsuspecting parents and caregivers, who in many cases are scrambling for answers to difficult school situations. Little do these family members and caregivers realize that myths and storytelling mask adult-centric, theoretical priorities that have little to do with the immediate or long-term learning requirements of students. The goal within this chapter is to discuss the tall tales, grassroots stories, university fables, and privatization myths that develop into free market gossip. This discussion illustrates that free market storytelling augments the shell game that obscures the enduring negative intents and effects of stealth-schooling.

TALL TALES

Before privatization myths emerged, a tall tale was invented about traditional public education. The gist of this tale is that traditional public education is an institutional dinosaur that deserves the apocalyptic meteor of reform because this creature is inefficiency at its bureaucratic, governmental worst (Chubb and Moe, 1990).

Like any tall tale worth telling, this one brings the remarkable hero, privatization, to the forefront, and the day is saved with reasoning straight out of the free market guidebook for stealth-schooling: "If the current system does, indeed, provide education to children inefficiently, then by increasing choice (which should induce competition), one can, theoretically, improve student achievement without significantly increasing public expenditures" (Rouse and Barrow, 2008, p. 1).

This wouldn't make a very good tale, however, if there weren't twists and turns in the plot line. As it turns out, mechanisms appear as schooling efficiency personified. Throughout the telling of this whopper, the heinous villain (traditional public education) is defeated by efficiency. Privatization proponents script a plot line in which mechanisms inspire the competitive nature of markets to save the day by distributing resources with greater efficiency than any bureaucratic monopoly could muster (Hess, 2010; Rouse and Barrow, 2008).

GRASSROOTS GOSSIP

Privatization advocates also share gossip about the alleged grassroots origin of choice education. However, if stealth-schooling is a grassroots movement, then Mount Rushmore is a sculpted pebble. Privatization, its mechanisms, and stealth-schooling usually originate not from humble grassroots but from the likes of ALEC, Americans for Prosperity, K-12 Inc., and other foundations, institutions, and businesses.

Individual marketeers who provide funding for these networks are "'a bunch of rich people who you can count on maybe two hands who have an inordinate impact. It's all about the money. It's not a function of anything else'" (Mayer, 2017, pp. 212–213). The tendency to invent stories about the origins of privatization and stealth-schooling extends to these tremendously wealthy ideologues who use free market gossip to hide their financial influence.

The *New York Times* discovered, for instance, that a purported grassroots movement in the 1990s "was in fact the product of a Washington-based group calling itself Citizens for Congressional Reform, which was started with hundreds of thousands of dollars from David Koch" (Mayer, 2017, p. 219).

UNIVERSITY FABLES

The forces arrayed to destroy traditional public education are dedicated to the proposition that less government is the best government. This belief eventuates in the premise that traditional public education is not only an unnecessary expenditure but an example of governmental overreach (Mayer, 2017). One way that free market schooling mavens attempt to subvert government overreach is by swamping universities across the US with a tidal wave of cash.

University Fable Factories

The Hoover Institution at Stanford University, the Mercatus Center at George Mason University, the Cato Institute, and the Heritage Foundation are among the university entities endowed with hefty contributions from marketeers. These well-funded entities reward investors with impressions and coded visions about the virtues of choice schooling, based on spurious research. What amounts to university-based fable factories spew forth research and op-ed pieces that lend the appearance of legitimate scientific inquiry to the myths of privatization (Mayer, 2017, p. 210).

Where There's a WILL There's a Free Market Fable

The power of copious amounts of cash linked with ideological zeal enables non-university research to mimic the storyline of university fables. The Wisconsin Institute for Law and Liberty (WILL), which is operated by the Bradley Foundation, generated a 2017 document purporting to demonstrate the superior academic effectiveness of stealth-schooling in Milwaukee compared to traditional public education in that city (Bielke, 2017).

Scholars from universities unaffiliated with any free market network or foundation, however, analyzed the report from WILL and found its research so flawed as to make its assertions and conclusions meaningless (Bielke, 2017). A defense of traditional public education cannot ignore the ideological stream of consciousness flowing from university fable factories to substantiate stealth-schooling while denigrating traditional public education.

A Free Market University-Legislature Union

University fables also emerge in connections between state-supported institutions of higher education and ALEC-friendly legislatures. For instance, Indiana's ALEC-influenced state legislature passed a bill in 2018 giving full control of a public-school district to Ball State University. The bill removed the locally elected school board of the Muncie (Indiana) Community Schools and replaced it with a board appointed by the university.

The new board is appointed by the trustees of the university, and its members do not have to live in the school district. Further, this university-legislature-originated fable leaves the now-privatized school district subject to only twenty-nine of the laws regulating traditional public education in Indiana (Smith, 2018). While the students and citizens of the school district wait, the new board of education and its appointed superintendent are taking two years to plan their implementation of free market schooling. In the meantime, little input is sought from either the university's teachers college or the educators who serve Muncie students each day. Choice is alive and well in this arrangement, but choice, again, is imposed, inspired by the free market, and political.

DISAPPEARING IN A CLOUD OF SMOKE

Advocates for choice schooling are so mesmerized by reform, efficiency, and less government that when data contradicts tales, stories, and fables about free market heroes, the once-upon-a-time importance of various story lines can become a matter for far, far away.

For instance, substantive national data about the failure of privatization to establish significantly better academic performance means that privatization storytellers deliberately remove student achievement from their plot (Hess, 2010). Also subject to disappearing in a cloud of smoke after a wave of the privatization storyteller's magic wand is the promise that choice schools close when they do not deliver robust levels of student achievement or any other promises made in the free market.

Marketeers readily share the myth that choice schools shut down if they do not survive the competition endemic to the free market. The efficiencies that are supposed to occur when choice schools close are, themselves, fairy tales when "despite low test scores, failing charter schools often have powerful and persuasive supporters in their communities who feel strongly that shutting down *this* school does not serve the best interests of currently enrolled students" (CREDO, 2009, p. 8).

When choice schools fail children academically, but failure is not convenient—politically and/or financially—marketeers submit a substitute happy ending. Data disappears, inept stealth-schools stay open, and failure, itself, disappears. Negative effects on students are edited out of free market schooling stories because they do not substantiate the glories of less government, the wizardry of competition, and the wonderland of excellence in choice education.

A STORYTELLER'S DREAM: VIRTUAL SCHOOLING

It is possible for those who tell fables about context of the free market to sound plausible and attractive to parents and caregivers whose first and best concern is the well-being and successful future of their children. An appeal to parents and caregivers based on the impressions of privatization like "choice" or "rights" or "freedom" conjures up an attractive picture of free market schooling. But the impressions rendered by the vocabulary of choice are the equivalent of a come-on from a carnival barker because, after the money is paid, the fantasies featured outside the tent do not live up to the realities inside the tent.

Outside the tent of privatization, for instance, something as glitzy and technology infused as online or virtual schooling sounds great to parents/caregivers and their children. Many are enticed with come-on stories of working at an individual pace with a rigorous academic curriculum at home in a safe environment. But inside the tent of virtual schooling, marketeers, ALEC members, and online schooling vendors offer up profit and free market misdirection, instead of teaching and learning. Corporate entities operating online stealth-schools for profit do so at the expense of students by "hiring teachers who are not certified, by hiring them at very low wages, and also by hiring a lot of tutors instead of teachers" (Elder, 2014).

Because states pay online education providers the same amount per student as traditional public schools, a significant profit is available regardless of abysmal quality or low-level information processing provided by online teaching and learning. Beneficiaries of this online circus are often those who create it in the first place. Tennessee's legislation that established online education, for example, was introduced by two legislators who were members of ALEC. The bill was introduced after it was written by two additional ALEC members, one a lobbyist for Connections Academy and the other with K-12, Inc. (Underwood and Mead, 2012).

Once virtual free market schooling is available, money changes hands. Pennsylvania provides a case in point where, in 2009, the state paid over $300 million tax dollars to cyber charter schools (Elder, 2014). Ohio's largest virtual school reaped profits despite terribly low student attendance rates that prompted state authorities to demand repayment of tens of millions of dollars from the company operating the school (Hefling, 2018a).

THREE MYTHS OF THE MARKETEERS

Marketeers place their faith in three myths to rationalize the value of and need for stealth-schooling in the United States. These myths are told time and again to convince the public that stealth-schooling works. These three—the myth of quality learning, the myth of spectacular efficiency, and the myth of alignment with America's needs/future—provide information about and insight into the tactics and intentions behind the attack on traditional public education. When free market adherents employ these myths, traditional public education colleagues can exploit the flaws in these tales for self-defense purposes.

The Myth of Quality Learning

Free market adherents generate an elaborate myth about high-level learning in choice schools. Even though there is no data to support this, the mythic hero known as *reform* is invoked as the presence that gives accuracy to this data-free concoction. The hollow core of the myth of quality learning in the free market is symbolized by information about reform in New Orleans (Gabor, 2015).

After Hurricane Katrina, New Orleans completed the implementation of a charter school makeover for almost 100 percent of the city's school system. Initial academic data emerging from this makeover gave rise to stories of robust improvement in student test proficiency and college entry rates. But the curtain that free market schooling in New Orleans stood behind to make this dubious claim was pulled aside to expose the myth of quality learning.

Behind the curtain, it turns out that significant numbers of students did not enroll in charter schools, which meant that achievement data shared from the early days of the New Orleans charter tsunami represented an insignificant portion of the city's student population. Next, principals at these schools took steps to "disconnect" poorly performing students from school attendance, which meant that those students least likely to demonstrate academic prowess were not allowed to attend when the required achievement tests were given.

Finally, city schools formerly labeled by the state with an "F" were given a "T" (for *Turnaround*) once a facility was transformed into a charter. This sleight-of-hand meant that negative academic results for entire schools were never reported (Gabor, 2015).

The myth of quality learning is not just a New Orleans phenomenon. Across the US, free market schools do not generate superior student academic performance. The 2009 CREDO study found that 83 percent of charter schools had math gains that were indistinguishable from or worse than those of traditional public schools. "This study reveals in unmistakable terms that, in the aggregate, charter students are not faring as well as their TPS counterparts" (CREDO, 2009, p. 6). The analysis of data from this study further indicated that "charter schools are not advancing the learning gains of their students as much as traditional public schools" (CREDO, 2009, p. 9).

The voucher system funded by the federal government, reverses the theme of this same myth. An independent study found negative academic effects for students attending Washington's elementary voucher schools whether those children previously attended a low- or high-performing traditional public school (Green, E. L., 2017).

The Myth of Spectacular Efficiency

Free market proponents relish the big myth that choice schooling is spectacularly efficient. Several aspects of this myth, however, portray a grisly narrative worthy of the original unsanitized fables written by the Brothers Grimm. Instead of spectacular efficiency and a happily-ever-after, the myth of spectacular efficiency is all about:

- Providing state tax dollars (in the form of either vouchers or tax credits) to families whose socioeconomic status reveals no need for state support. This monstrous inefficiency increases the cost of education without creating identifiable efficiency at any of the parochial schools that benefit the most from this tax-dollar funding.

    This outcome is a fairy tale that only a marketeer could love. In this plot, efficiency means the Sheriff of Nottingham gets to keep his ill-gotten gains because there is no Robin Hood.

- Using a dollars-per-pupil model to fund education. Free market advocates often sell this funding model by sloganeering about tax dollars following the child. In most cases this alleged efficiency results in a plague of fewer state dollars following students in traditional public schools (as in Indiana and Michigan) while larger dollar totals follow each child enrolled in stealth-schools.

    This per-pupil funding gambit has been labeled "a 'long game,' a means of paying lip service to greater equality while creating a 'more efficient, market-oriented system where money follows students'" (Binelli, 2017, p. 7). Refusing enrollment in choice schools to any student for any reason or creating enrollment difficulties for unwanted students, efficiency in stealth-schooling is based on nothing less than exclusionary enrollment.

- Even before thinking about the possibility of enrollment in choice education, unwanted, undesirable, or unacceptable students are subject to this so-called efficiency. Cinderella's stepsisters and free market schooling are equally interested in limiting who attends the royal ball.

  In the world of stealth-schooling, special education students, minority students, and English-language learners are frequently unwanted. Even if a stealth-school might accept an otherwise excluded student, families from lower socioeconomic cohorts are often unable to enroll their children because choice schools frequently locate in or near more affluent neighborhoods to ensure robust profit.

  The myth of efficiency of privatization is such that stealth-schooling royalty can enroll, but unwanted students are consigned to the free market's version of the "pit of misery," aka traditional public education.

- Devouring tax dollars that would otherwise be used to satisfy state constitutional imperatives for universal and free education. Adequacy of education—quality learning environments for all students called for in each state's constitution—is abandoned when the myth of spectacular efficiency creates funding shortfalls for traditional public education.

  More affluent school districts in states where this happens may pass local referenda or approve other local taxation mechanisms in response to decreasing state funding. Poor school districts have the same authority to bring tax increases to their voters but are much less likely to gain the electorate's approval for necessary additional funding via bond, levy, or referendum.

  Because legislators are swayed by myths of the free market, the impact of privatization falls heavily upon the students and communities least able to accommodate or recover from the financial impact of state funding shortfalls. Instead of efficiency, this privatization myth is all about a troll who gobbles up tax dollars to deny financial stability and equality throughout traditional public education.

The Myth of Alignment with America's Future

This myth is told between the lines of impressions shared by free market schooling proponents. The advocates of stealth-schooling encase any number of impressions and coded messages in their tales. These messages share ideological assumptions about America. Perhaps the most egregious of these messages is that US democracy requires a free market for education to benefit the nation's most privileged individuals and businesses.

The extent to which privatization misrepresents the relationship between education and democracy and the serious problems that this can cause in the future can be anticipated in a brief consideration of the history of this relationship. Empowering democracy and the American Dream is a longtime objective of traditional public education in that "the goal of education was an informed and intelligent citizenry capable of making good choices with respect to the leaders and policies of the nation and the society" (Covaleskie, 2007, p. 38).

Self-Defense in the Three Myths

From the myths generated in support of free market schooling emerge several self-defense strategies for traditional public educators. For example, the commitment of state constitutions to universal public education, the establishment of statutes or rules to carry out this responsibility, and the specification therein of standards that require universal education with equality under the law are carried out daily within the time-honored baseline of the public good supported by professional practice in traditional public education (Covaleskie, 2007; Dewey, 1916; Long, 2018).

Traditional public education and US democracy embody the conjunction of higher order cognition, collaboration and individual initiatives derived from knowing how to think, and the capacity to improve and grow continuously to balance individual and public goods. These capacities emerge from learning experiences fashioned within points of practice. The purpose of traditional public education and the function exercised to realize this purpose generate data and examples that traditional public education colleagues should put to good use for self-defense.

CHOOSING BETWEEN THE GOOD OF THE MANY AND THE POWER OF THE FEW

The primary purpose of traditional public education provides the opportunities necessary to take teaching, learning, and our nation beyond the historic malfeasance represented by prejudice and bigotry. Devoted to the value of each student, traditional public education invests in the greater good persistently, even though this outcome is still on the horizon. However, an American future handcuffed to the myths of the free market puts the power of citizenship, the rights due to all citizens, and the necessity for continuous improvement into the hands of a limited few dedicated to adult-centric and economic benefits from the implementation of free market schooling. No myth that envisions such an ending deserves to become a how-to manual for educating the future of America.

Once in place, these impressions masquerade as outcomes of value to students and give privatization advocates carte blanche to manufacture a self-fulfilling prophesy. The ballyhooed benefits of choice schooling are based upon reports generated by these same advocates that parents and caregivers are more satisfied with choice schooling than they are with traditional public schools (Hess, 2010). This self-serving, tautological, network-funded, ideologically anchored schooling charade develops, as Diane Ravitch observes, out of the devotion of privatization ideologues to FUD: fear, uncertainty, and doubt (Moyers, 2014).

The Mythic Character Valued by Marketeers—FUD: Fear, Uncertainty, and Doubt

FUD is the character lurking behind the scenes in many of the tales of free market schooling. FUD is featured—whether in a major role or a cameo appearance—in choice schooling fables to instill misgivings about traditional public education. FUD can appeal to parents and caregivers whose personal prejudices mingle with concern for their children. The study of FUD as a phenomenon—known as *agnotology*—is relevant to advocates for traditional public education who must be aware that "whole industries devote themselves to sowing public misinformation and doubt" (Moyers, 2014).

The privatization agenda crawling with my-side bias markers (less government, lower taxes, and self-aggrandizement by wealthy individuals and corporations) sows FUD into a montage that disparages traditional public schools (Hefling, 2017). The impressions visited upon society by privatization adherents allege that vouchers, tax credits, education savings plans, and charter schools create schooling that is more safe, more family friendly, more ideologically beneficial, and more child centered than traditional public education.

As early as 1990, a relatively mild invocation of FUD appeared in an ideological piece alleging that traditional public schools were little more than bureaucratic, inefficient, governmental boondoggles with little to offer students, parents, caregivers, or society (Chubb and Moe, 1990). Almost thirty years later, FUD plays a much more dominant role in the myths told on behalf of free market schooling. For instance, when a for-profit charter management company took over the Highland Park school district in the Detroit area, a Michigan think tank produced a pro-choice schooling video that "opened with slow-panning, verite-horror-film footage of derelict public school buildings, including a shot of a filthy toilet" (Binelli, 2017, p. 5).

The devotion of privatization proponents to misinformation and doubt is further exemplified in comments from a free market schooling proponent addressed to a group of traditional public school leaders that conjured up this hypothetical public school scenario: "'Right now a student at school is stepping over rats, breathing in mold, and dodging fists'" (Hefling, 2018b).

In a digital age where online gossip becomes truth and evidence simply because it exists, FUD about traditional public education "makes people so desperate that they will seek out unproven alternatives. It makes the public gullible when they hear phony claims about miracle [choice] schools" (Moyers, 2014). Although some dismiss FUD as a relatively harmless practice adopted from American business, scholars indicate that FUD is nothing less than the deliberate cultural production of ignorance.

FUD appeals to privatization proponents as an investment in structuring social problems aided and abetted by the deliberate cultural production of ignorance. Proponents of school choice deploy FUD impressions to prey upon and exacerbate parental concerns about what's best for their children.

WHAT TRADITIONAL PUBLIC EDUCATORS SHOULD DO: COMMUNICATE FACTS!

Gathered to support the agenda of the free market, a host of myths, tales, and stories confront traditional public education in the United States. FUD, the cultural production of ignorance, the primacy of self-interest, my-side bias, the structuring of social problems—all must be accounted for to defend traditional public education and to preserve the opportunity for future generations of US students to learn *how to think*.

Self-defense must incorporate as much factual, student-focused, communication as possible. To this end, traditional public educators must share with parents, caregivers, stakeholders, policymakers, and school partners, a host of communications that emphasize:

- *We care about your child's thinking.* This phrase conveys two standout characteristics of traditional public education: caring for *all* children and professional expertise about *how to think*, which benefits the future of all children.

    Making statements that share examples from classrooms about these realities tells parents and caregivers how creativity, intelligence of all kinds, compassion, humor, civility, social justice, and cognitive behaviors within responsive cognition are at the heart of teaching and learning every day. Putting these outcomes into communications to describe classrooms allows family members to gather the facts and, thus, "get the message" about traditional public education.

- *Your child's future is today!* Traditional public educators focus on each child. And the everyday teaching and learning that a child experiences in each classroom is all about fulfilling individual potential.

The rich potential of each student is the future nurtured by the primary purpose of traditional public education. Colleagues know that *how to think* is an essential resource for any and all future positive contributions students make to themselves and US society.

With this in mind, the proposition that the primary purpose of traditional public education is *how to think* does not assume that all students are college bound. On the contrary! *How to think* is an essential resource for every student in any and every future and occupation they may choose. Whether as a future welder, ballerina, corporate executive, carpenter, engineer, ironworker, homemaker, farmer, musician, lawyer, nurse, technology entrepreneur, call-center specialist, or any other role in any other field, all students deserve *how to think* as a resource.

It's important to tell parents and caregivers about the excellence that emerges from *how to think*, and that excellence is expressed in the life of their child(ren) in a multitude of different ways. All students can be successful in their lives and make positive, constructive, and enriching choices when they know *how to think*. The economic and personal futures of all individual students that are enhanced in traditional public education deserve to be front and center when parents and caregivers hear and see how educators serve their child(ren) each day.

- *Identify my-side bias in privatization.* The ideology that ALEC represents and that free market schooling espouses is the epitome of my-side bias. Privatization claims to seek benefits for students but data does not support this hyperbole. My-side bias thinking thrives because free market adherents profess that privatization and its mechanisms are ends unto themselves (Lubienski, 2013).

  This means that students, families, and communities are an afterthought, from the perspective of free market theory. Mandating mechanisms that bring stealth-schooling to American society is its own reward for marketeers.

  In addition, looking beyond the hyperbole, FUD, and impressions, the beneficiaries of choice education are often the management companies that operate choice schools; the so-called entrepreneurs whose real estate and banking businesses profit from real estate gimmicks associated with school property; ideologues whose desire for less government is satisfied when mechanisms unrelated to teaching and learning are created; and the networks whose purpose is to promote their own profit and personal wealth despite devastating consequences for equality, adequacy, and social justice.

- *Distribute classroom expectations.* The expectations and standards and habits of mind embedded in quality instruction for students in traditional public education classrooms should be "posted" and explained not only for students but also for parents and caregivers.

  Posting a primary purpose and examples of quality professional practice to social media or classroom sites helps family members stay up-to-date with their child's learning experiences. These explanations and examples give parents and caregivers facts and examples to use when asking their children, "What did you do in school today?" In place of this generic question (which is often followed with the quick, if inaccurate, response, "*Nothing*"), encourage parents and caregivers to ask specific questions about habits of mind, instructional activities, or expectations presented during any day's classroom journey toward *how to think*.

  Encourage parents and caregivers to be specific when asking about the day's events. "What are you studying in (math, music, social studies, science, etc.)?" gives a prompt from which a dialogue can develop about learning. This kind of immediate dialogue and information about teaching and learning is an important way to share the value of traditional public education.

WHAT EDUCATORS SHOULD DO: SPEAK THE LANGUAGE OF SUCCESSFUL PRACTICE

To make mincemeat of the myths invented by free market devotees requires a focus on the value of our *how to think*. This focus should emphasize *the language of successful practice.*

Our schools, grade-level teams, subject-area departments, and all colleagues should persistently include in their language key words and phrases that convey the data-based virtues of public education while emphasizing a commitment to bettering the lives of all children. *How to think* and successful intelligence represent, after all, the grand goal of students learning how to interact productively and civilly with other likeminded and not-likeminded students from wonderfully diverse backgrounds.

In addition, traditional public educators need to articulate clearly how quality instruction will change and respond if students demonstrate learning that is not consistent with instructional goals. The language of successful practice should:

- *Emphasize* vocabulary and phrases such as: *your* child, *productive future*, learning, happy, *high quality*, safe; *growing*, succeeding, *making progress* (give specific examples), continuous improvement, *creative*, thoughtful, *organized*, resilient, *persistent*, honest, *self-reliant*.

These and many other affirmative terms are the baseline of the language of successful practice. This vocabulary is only the beginning, however, and it must be accompanied by data and descriptions of the learning, interactions, and behavior to demonstrate student success. In this way, educators spotlight the intent and effect of professional practice, using practical everyday terms linked with data.

At the same time, this language shares data and details with parents/caregivers about how quality professional practices grow the thinking behaviors (including brain development throughout a coordinated and comprehensive educational program) of their child. The details about free market schooling shared throughout this book indicate that now is the time to ramp up efforts to speak the language of student success.

Placing these examples in front of as many parents, caregivers, and citizens as possible does not add a time-consuming task that further entangles colleagues in the web of existing mandates for public school colleagues. Rather, when regular communications with parents and caregivers incorporate examples of success that are linked to *how to think*, educators have existing material to emphasize the excellence of traditional public education to a variety of different "audiences" in the community.

- *Relay these affirmations* via existing teacher, classroom, department, grade-level, and/or school websites to magnify the focus of quality instruction. Emphasizing how educators work to support, enrich, and nurture the child/young person of each parent or caregiver ensures that the primary responsibility of traditional public education is on the radar of all adults who care for each student.

- *Post short classroom videos*, with permission from parents/caregivers, in which students talk about their thinking based on what's been taught in class. These illustrations bring life to professional practice and allow educators to expound authentically with school communities through the language of success.

    Students talking about habits of mind in conjunction with classroom projects, assignments, and tasks gives parents and caregivers a realistic glimpse of the capacities of their children and the power of traditional public education.

- *Put the language of success* "in play" when a high school in a school district has a radio station or a drama department or a speech team or technology-connected classes or access to an educational TV channel. Incorporating the language of success using these formats brings real examples and up-to-date information to the school community.

The importance of sharing clear, frequent, and positive examples about the successful outcomes of traditional public education cannot be overstated as colleagues work to undo fabrications, myths, and misdirection. In this case, the best defense is a frequent, honest, student-centered, data-driven offense dedicated to sharing specific information about student success.

- *Heed the implications* of Diane Ravitch's observation that free marketeers have stolen the concept of reform and made it their own in a way that implies that traditional public education requires eradication (Moyers, 2014).

Traditional public education practices and outcomes should be explained to reveal that for all students, the future is now. Instead of mechanisms and thinking-as-rejection, traditional public education understands each student as excellence personified. *How to think* gives traditional public educators ownership of the language of success.

THIRTEEN

Policymaking: Is That a Light at the End of the Tunnel?

To burst the policy bubble established across the United States by adherents of free market theory, it is time for traditional public educators to attend to policymaking. Attending to policymaking may mean that some colleagues run for office. Attending to policymaking for all colleagues means applying cognitive behaviors at the core of professional practice to dialogue with legislators, business leaders, and others in defense of traditional public education.

Policymakers need to hear from educators in traditional public education and from parents/caregivers that a return to full support for traditional public education is a nonnegotiable so that all children and young people will experience learning that engages with habits of mind to "build a capacity for judgment" (Higgins and Knight Abowitz, 2011, p. 379). The capacity for judgment nurtures a sense of the public as "a space in which new senses of 'we' could be formed across divisions and where judgments about the common good could be slowly constructed out of diverse perspectives without this being preempted by an aggregation of individual interests" (p. 372).

Forthright action devoted to policymaking by traditional public education thwarts the wide range of problems, mistakes, dangers, and failures delivered by free market theory to students, parents/caregivers, and communities throughout the United States. Time—the reign of free market mythology spans more than a half century since its first articulation by Milton Friedman (1955)—lays bare the fundamental mismatch between stealth-schooling and American democracy.

This chapter provides insights into and impetus for a paradigm shift about policymaking. Policy is a tool for self-defense of traditional public education with the potential to end the thought-free and adult-centric policymaking that foists free market schooling on US students.

GLIMMERS OF HOPE?

Although many policymakers do not foster in any significant way the stalwart support that traditional public education deserves, the dismal outcomes associated with free market schooling may be responsible for a few glimmers of policymaking support for the purpose and quality of traditional public education. Cracks in the façade of allegiance to unregulated implementation of free market schooling can be found.

One bill introduced in the Indiana Senate during the 2018 legislative session, for instance, required the Indiana Department of Education to establish rules "to prevent charter school organizers from committing financial or enrollment 'fraud, waste and abuse'" (Cavazos, 2018). This bill also proposed that entities in the Hoosier State permitted to authorize charter schools—universities, mayors, and school districts—could not offer a charter to any organizer if students in the organizer's existing charters are not achieving academically (Cavazos, 2018).

Perhaps realizing the extent to which free market schooling underserves its students while hoodwinking its legislative supporters, this same bill required that data supplied by charter authorizers prove the academic benefits that students attain from free market schooling.

In the Indiana House of Representatives, a different bill offered during the 2018 legislative session attended to the fiscal flimflam that can accompany stealth-schooling. Noting that Indiana's charter schools are "'a little out of control,'" the sponsor of this bill took aim at the murky financial activities that occur when charter schools and authorizers continue to collaborate and continue to operate, even though the school(s) fail students academically.

Not only do charter schools continue to take students under these conditions and receive per-pupil funding, but "'authorizers get a cut of their funding, so there's a lot of incentive for authorizers to create these new schools'" (Cavazos, 2018). This bill sought to prohibit an authorizer from approving a new school if an existing school operated by the same organizer earned a grade of D or F from the state for two consecutive years.

ALL THAT GLIMMERS IS NOT GOLD

Glimmers of hope from policymakers, however, are not the norm. The effect of myths, storytelling, and self-aggrandizement in free market ideology is so powerful that most policymakers revert to supporting context without regard for data that reveals inefficiency or academic ineptitude in choice schooling.

In Indiana, adherence to free market theory, network-designed model bills, and the emerging status quo of privatization represents just the kind of uniformity of policy making necessary to avoid research and data. In the Hoosier State, free market proponents in the legislature "forged ahead without any hard proof of success, broadening the pool of students eligible for vouchers. What's more, no cap exists on the number of students who can receive a voucher" (Schneider, 2017, p. 3A).

As one Indiana lawmaker who supports privatization put it, "'I always go back to the fact that we're trying to empower parents here to say what's the best choice for your child. We're doing it for people who cannot afford an option other than a public school'" (Schneider, 2017, p. 4A). The apparent inability of so many policymakers to engage with traditional public education colleagues in discourse is represented by a staunch unwillingness to recognize the disconnection between the adult-centric ideology of the free market and the pursuit of *how to think* on behalf of students.

POLICY PROMOTES POOR PAY IN THE FREE MARKET

Paying attention to policymaking in defense of, and for the restoration of, traditional public education may seem like a fool's errand. After all, the preponderance of evidence about policymaking in states around the US illustrates that ALEC-connected, well-funded, academically disassociated policies distort the influence of traditional public education in the lives of US students. The overwhelming influence of privatization proponents and their networks puts traditional public educators in a bind.

Examples of policymaking support for the ascension of free market schooling and the demise of traditional public education abound. Among the most incendiary examples, policymaking siphons dollars away from traditional public education and in so doing, decreases the salaries of traditional public education colleagues. Data from the National Center for Education Statistics shows examples of the decline in teacher pay (adjusted for inflation) since 1999–2000 from Arizona (–10 percent) to Michigan (–11.5 percent), and from North Carolina (–12 percent) to Colorado (–15 percent) (Picchi, 2018).

The policies emanating from free market theory devotees establish lower cost in government by reducing pay for traditional public educators. The free market's preoccupation with less government has a devastating impact on traditional public educators. In Indiana, traditional public educators have seen a 16 percent pay decrease since 1999–2000 accompanied by an obvious cause-and-effect problem throughout the state for traditional public schools that have "trouble finding enough qualified teachers to fill classrooms" (Picchi, 2018).

GLIMMERS FOR SELF-DEFENSE

Throughout the US, the long-term effects of policymakers' allegiance to the implementation of the free market of schooling are raising awareness among traditional public education colleagues. In 2018, statewide teacher walkouts in West Virginia, Oklahoma, Arizona, and Kansas occurred with the intent of influencing legislators and policymakers to undo statutes and policies strangling traditional public education (Hefling, 2018c). These overt and dramatic efforts to influence and improve policy that affects traditional public education arose, in part, out of woeful disparities between state policies.

Awareness of the damage done by free market policymaking is fueled by comparisons of state funding for traditional public education. For instance, the average annual salary for a colleague in New York is almost $80,000, but colleagues in South Dakota, the state with the lowest average annual salary, earn barely $43,000 annually (Picchi, 2018). Across the US, traditional public educators in twenty-nine states earn less than they did at the turn of the twenty-first century; meanwhile, "the cost of living has increased almost 50 percent since then" (Picchi, 2018).

When policy and statute are used as a free market battering ram, the day-to-day attack on traditional public education takes a toll on colleagues and their families and on students and their families. Falling wages and inadequate attention to *how to think* are deficits that reduce the economic and academic potential of vast numbers of American adults and even larger numbers of American students whose lives are wrapped up in traditional public education.

The self-defense efforts initiated in 2018 by traditional public educators and their families to reverse negative policymaking suggest several additional ways to affect policymaking so that decision making at the state level is directed toward full support for traditional public education:

- *Network locally.* The information and data about the myriad successes of traditional public education that colleagues already share with stakeholders, parents/caregivers, and school partners should be shared with other schools and school districts. Policy often emerges from successes, data, or shared concerns.

  When traditional public education colleagues compare notes, they create opportunities to amass information and data-connected perspectives that can inform policymakers and counteract the fairy tales told by privatization proponents. Local networks need to communicate frequently so that the effect of policies can be assessed and so that this effect can be shared among communities.

- *Network nationally.* Influencing national policy with data related to the necessity to improve the pursuit of *how to think* can energize the jump from local to national policymaking when educators incorporate actions and communications employed at the local level. Using existing links among organizations devoted to excellence in traditional public education and/or inspiring spontaneous "hashtag" constituencies allows important ideas for improved policy to have a national voice.

- *Network "across the aisle."* Too often, traditional public educators undo good ideas or directions for policy because of adversarial postures adopted between the different roles within the profession. Self-imposed, this professional dysfunction often exists along a dividing line between teachers and school leaders. However, traditional public educators have much more in common than they have issues or perspectives that may separate them.

    Although this does not mean that agreement on all matters is possible, it does suggest that what amounts to a *collaboration zone* should be identified so that teachers and administrators can work together on ideas, concepts, rules, statutes, and policies dedicated to crafting function, purpose, and increased funding throughout traditional public education.

- *Network with allies.* It's important to remember that there are policymakers and other leaders who support the transformative impact of traditional public education. These allies should be points of frequent contact when educators share information and ideas relevant to policies that affect the profession.

    Communicating with leaders and policymakers who understand the vibrant contributions of traditional public education to students and US society allows these allies to dialogue with other leaders and policymakers using data.

    Because continuous improvement and maturing perspectives are rooted in function and the primary purpose of traditional public education, all professional networks should carry data about the impact of these into coordinated efforts to establish policies that deliver full support for comprehensive traditional public education.

- *Dig for accurate information about policy.* Policy and state statutes often develop without much fanfare. The effort it takes to ferret out new or emerging policy at the state level is usually undertaken by only a few individuals or organizations. Too often, colleagues perceive policymaking and state legislative antics as a distraction or, worse, unrelated to professional practice at the local level.

Nothing could be further from the truth. Traditional public educators should network actively with organizations, agencies, individuals, and state entities immersed in policymaking while keeping an eye on the accuracy and impact of data, information, and directions generated by these groups. Accurate data, when it's shared across networks, sheds light on emerging policy so that the potential for a positive or negative impact on traditional public education can be evaluated and communicated.

Maximizing the chance to work and communicate with allies and adversaries when statutes or policies are "in process" means that ALEC and other free market proponents have less of an opportunity to impose "it's a done deal" for policy at the state level.

- *Encourage policy canaries.* Canaries were used long ago in mines to warn miners about the accumulation of life-threatening gases. In the same way, colleagues within local and school-associated networks need to be designated to read and watch for information from as many sources as possible that signal policy threats to traditional public education.

  Traditional public educators need colleagues who sift through the mountain of policy-related information to ensure that developing regulations and statutes are not lost amid the often byzantine procedures of state legislatures, only to surface when it's too late.

  These policy canaries will research and read a great deal that has little or no relation to policy for the profession. But when policies are discovered that impact traditional public education—for better or for worse—these colleagues can rally fellow educators to engage state leaders to support policy dedicated to what's best for students: strong support for comprehensive traditional public education.

A POLICY PARADIGM FOR TRADITIONAL PUBLIC EDUCATION

Data, information, and quality are essential elements if traditional public educators are to illuminate the pathway to policies that support and improve the profession. Networking to share data, information, and quality is essential if educators want to turn dialogue about the facts relevant to quality into effective tools for policymaking.

Failure to attend to networking or failure to network with accurate data and information about professional practices in traditional public education could turn the potential for policymaking as a proverbial light at the end of the tunnel into the headlight of a free market policy locomotive advancing to roll over *how to think,* quality instruction, and student futures.

Policymaking for a future of continuous improvement of function during the student-centric journey toward *how to think* can be initiated through a comparison of existing state policies with positive examples from other states to demonstrate policies that should replace those with negative effects on traditional public education. Policymakers and politicians need to hear from as many positive voices as possible about how purpose and function craft better futures for all students and how policy supporting traditional public education is the means to those better futures.

Under the auspices of *how to think,* professional practice incorporates both model-of and model-for instruction to bring about the most effective function possible on behalf of our students. Under the auspices of *how to think,* traditional public educators have the responsibility and the opportunity to change the wayward direction of current free market–friendly policies. Policy makers deserve and need a thorough, civil, and data-filled environment in which traditional public educators help them see the better future for students that traditional public education provides.

WHAT EDUCATORS SHOULD DO: RALLY SUPPORT FOR TRADITIONAL PUBLIC EDUCATION

Free market theory is a schooling boondoggle fueled by financing that benefits corporations, networks, and well-heeled plutocrats. Absconding with dollars that should be spent on student learning in traditional public education, privatization proponents mock the public good and the value-added nature of a fully realized democracy.

More than 60 percent of those responding to a prominent national poll, when given ample information, indicated opposition to using public funds to pay for private education (PDK, 2017). To defend against the run on the bank that drains funding for traditional public education and to defend against the policy manipulation that steals successful intelligence from US students, the self-defense of traditional public education must include building upon and increasing the support that educators already enjoy. To do this, several actions that require no additional funding (obviously, because educators have none) are available.

- *Follow the money!* All of America's children deserve an education adequate to their needs and adequate to the challenges and opportunities that the future will present to them. The misanthropic ideology that contradicts this fundamental premise of universal education and the debilitating impact of the dollars siphoned away from universal traditional public education to free market schooling should be broadcast widely among parents, caregivers, and citizens.

Since the ideology advanced by free market schooling proponents stipulates a defunding of public education, the details about underfunding in each school district are a vital fact to share and share again. In addition, local legislators and political leaders should be informed about the significant research finding that "states that send additional money to their lowest-income school districts see more academic improvement in those districts than states that don't" (Carey and Harris, 2016).

The link between underfunding student learning and policy that supports choice education should be put under a spotlight. Parents, caregivers, and community members need to know that the full measure of their tax dollars is not being used to support their child(ren). Parents, caregivers, and citizens need to know that research indicates that ample tax dollars *do* make a difference in traditional public education when it comes to delivering the quality learning that all US children and young people deserve (Carey and Harris, 2016).

- *Get the facts!* Ask specific questions to get the facts about state dollars that are diverted from traditional public education. Check with local print journalists for their "take" on this problem. Then, ask state legislators questions based on the information gathered about this misdirected funding. Ask specifically about who profits when traditional public education and its students lose.

  Once information is shared with parents, caregivers, colleagues, and citizens about the loss of state revenue, use the democratic process to ensure that the entire community collaborates to restore the money denied to its students.

- *Use the RTS facts!* It's important to introduce the concept of RTS (return to students) and keep it in front of state leaders and policymakers. Communications with state legislators and state political leaders need to ask for precise numbers about state funding for charters and vouchers.

  Data about per-pupil funding (to determine the amount provided for choice schooling compared with the amount provided for traditional public education) must be requested and, then, compared with numbers provided by local journalists and other reliable public sources. How does per-pupil funding for students in comprehensive traditional public education compare to per-pupil funding that supports free market schools?

  Precise numbers are needed, also, about tax credits and tax avoidance. Then, with numbers in hand, communicate with the school community about dollars taken away from students and lost to free market misdirection. Ask advocates to communicate with leaders about the necessity for restoring and increasing dollars to educate students in traditional public education. Lost funding, funding from the state given to ineffective and inefficient stealth-schools, must be restored to traditional public education to ensure the future of all students, their communities, the economy, and US democracy.

- *Follow the money in a different direction!* Charter schools provide banks and hedge funds with strong profit potential. Legislators, charter school authorizers, and charter school leaders should be asked about profit, debt, loans, and other opportunities for fiscal misadventure embedded in the state's statutory homage to privatization.

    Tax breaks may accrue to financial institutions for investing in charters. Combined with the knowledge vacuum about school financing that afflicts charter authorizers and charter school boards, tax credits and other fiscal machinery can be factors that accelerate profit rates for companies or fiscal malfeasance in choice schools and organizations (Binelli, 2017).

- *Share details from the state, the community.* In most cases, when free market schooling drains tax dollars away from public education, journalists at the local or state level pay attention. Utilizing state and local data detailed by journalists allows traditional public educators to illustrate the negative impact of stealth-schooling on students.

    When traditional public educators are upfront about the damage done by privatization's fiscal malpractice, a door is opened for parents, caregivers, and citizens to take the "next step" of insisting on redress of this situation with state legislators and other officials.

- *Explain fairness in relationship to public education.* Talking about fairness with state legislators and other officials—whether in person, by phone, or via written communication—gives a human face to the consequences of inadequate state funding for traditional public education. When it comes to the importance of state taxes devoted to students, illustrations from day-to-day learning that demonstrate how children and young people are being shortchanged by free market policy need to be shared.

- *Illustrate the real-world benefits of traditional public education.* The benefits of a comprehensive curriculum—including offerings in the performing and fine arts, vocational skills, business, family and consumer sciences, and physical education—and the benefits of a robust set of extra- and co-curricular offerings convey how traditional public education enriches the thinking and lives of all students.

Further, illustrations of equity, social justice, academic achievement, and other student successes in traditional public education demonstrate the proverbial tip of the educational iceberg; imagine, state leaders, what comprehensive traditional public education could achieve if fully funded!

In addition, the responsibility of the state to provide a fully funded quality education in traditional public schools (common schools referred to in state constitutions are a baseline for equity and equality often ignored or bypassed during the rush to privatization [Long, 2018]) should not be short-circuited by funneling monetary support to the free market of schooling.

- *Establish equity and equality as nonnegotiables.* Within school district budgets, traditional public school colleagues have accurate data about the impact of declining revenue on the futures of students. This data must be utilized to create an accurate and data-based picture for the school community and for legislators who serve the school community because lost funding signifies declining equity and equality in traditional public education (Herron and Fittes, 2017).

  Policymakers need to be informed about the research-based implications for students from adequate funding of traditional public education including "how long students stayed in school and how much they earned as adults" (Carey and Harris, 2016).

  Tragically, traditional public schools in low-income communities of referendum states have little recourse for recovery when dollars are siphoned away by ideology. Business-office officials in school districts should take the lead and articulate how the community is shortchanged by privatization.

- *Tell the story of traditional public education to the school community.* Each school and school district should "tell our story" to its community. The rationale for comprehensive traditional public education needs to be shared with those most affected by and most likely to listen to virtuousness: the local school community. Too often, public educators feel compelled to dialogue with individuals who have no actual connection with the community, its citizens, its children, or its schools.

  These disconnected individuals "arrive" at school, often via social media, with the sole intention of attacking, condemning, accusing, belittling, or shaming school activities, individuals, situations, or events. These correspondents usually have no connection with the school community and even less of a connection with accurate information about the issues, funding, successes, or concerns that the school community deals with. The tendency to use social media to disparage seems to be exacerbated by distance.

Responding to these self-important, self-righteous, and overtly false voices that do not represent the school community is a waste of time, unnecessary, enervating, and futile. Instead, when a problem or serious incident arises, giving the school community accurate information and telling what's being done in regard to the information eliminates FUD and provides the means for restoration of community connections for trust.

Consistently informing the school community about the best of the human condition residing in teaching and learning conveys dynamically the most likely behaviors occurring at any traditional public school.

Sharing accurate information about the disastrous fiscal impact of privatization is one way to defend traditional public education. Clear and accurate details that demonstrate the negative fiscal impact of privatization on students in each traditional public school give parents and caregivers fact-based resources to battle negative legislative or administrative actions at the state level.

To counter the impact of those who seek the destruction of traditional public schools, traditional public education colleagues must talk about how students and teachers are hurt by funding shortfalls, by negative policy, and by thinking-as-rejection created by the decisions of legislators and others smitten with the false promises and inequities delivered by free market thinking. Self-defense strategies of traditional public education colleagues must unmask and disarm the myth makers whose robber-baron ways debilitate and derail the public good.

FOURTEEN
The Self-Defense Responsibilities of Traditional Public Educators

Only two summative conclusions can arise from this discussion about a continuing assault on traditional public education in the United States. The first conclusion is that the efforts of proponents of the free market of schooling are an ongoing threat to all of America's students. The second conclusion is that the first best self-defense of traditional public education begins with the millions of colleagues who serve students in this transformative US institution.

A FIRST SUMMATIVE CONCLUSION

An impossible situation confronts students across the nation. Two perspectives—free market schooling and traditional public education—divide the educational landscape. Research indicates that free market adherents' dedication to less government undercuts students no matter where they enroll. However, with nine out of every ten US students attending traditional public schools, free market theory constitutes a specific assault on traditional public education. Moreover, the intents and outcomes of the free market of schooling segregate, undereducate, defund, marginalize, and restrict vast numbers of US students and their futures. This threat is nothing less than a danger to the future of democracy.

A SECOND SUMMATIVE CONCLUSION

The discussion undertaken in this book fosters a second summative conclusion: the millions of colleagues who serve all students throughout traditional public education in the United States are the first best line of self-defense against the assault by proponents of the free market of schooling. The purpose, function, and quality instruction riveted to traditional public education engage all students with the bright future they deserve: successful intelligence. The professional practices of traditional public education provide a treasure trove of cognitive behaviors that establish bright futures for all students.

Understanding these summative conclusions, however, constitutes just the beginning of the important insights required to thwart the negative impact of the free market of schooling while, at the same time, engaging with all the resources necessary to mount a stalwart self-defense of traditional public education. To end the adult-centric focus of free market thinking and to forestall the negative impact of thinking that equates free market mechanisms with teaching and learning requires that traditional public educators take account of a number of factors including the power of day-to-day professional practice.

SELF-DEFENSE BEGINS AND ENDS WITH QUALITY PRACTICE

Quality practice in traditional public education is anchored by *how to think*, its primary purpose. *How to think* puts all students in position to become knowledge builders capable of social justice in the choice of a balance between individual and public goods. On the other hand, the myths, oxymorons, and dangers embedded within free market schooling have little to do with advancing the thinking and futures of all students. If there is a primary purpose of free market schooling, it is the installation of mechanisms masquerading as schooling to allow the delivery of less cost and less government.

Free market proponents—a dizzying array of networks, foundations, and plutocrats—employ FUD, amorality of the market, dissemination of public misinformation, and my-side bias to reach objectives divorced from the lives, thinking, and futures of America's students. As a result, the free market of schooling presents an exclusively dominant narrative where freedom is accorded only to the privileged and where status is bestowed only on marketeers and other true believers in market theory. Compartmentalization of students, narrowing of the curriculum, entrapment in an age of assessment, addiction to "keeping score," fascination with fairy tales—all illuminate the misdirection of teaching and learning mired in the free market of schooling.

A focus on knowledge, cognitive process, and intelligence gives traditional public educators the wherewithal to engage students with learning habits of mind that enrich the interplay of layers of cognition in the brain. Responsive cognition, cognitive agency, and successful intelligence establish *positive liberty*, which Fraser-Burgess (2012) describes as a vast freedom expressed in individuals being ruled by their own reason.

Traditional public educators are not solely involved with self-defense. In addition, quality practice in traditional public education defends US democracy, the admixture of science and art, covenantal attachment, and balance. These strengths of traditional public education not only confront the dichotomies of US democracy but also prompt the necessity for majority educators to mediate identity. Valorizing the identity of all students and engaging the capabilities of all students gives traditional public education a powerful impact well beyond the stasis found in the context of free market schooling. The conjoint communicated experience that Dewey (1916) identifies as US democracy demands social justice, continuous improvement, and *how to think*.

The power of traditional public education lies, also, in the ethical non-negotiables that guide professional practice. To serve all students, traditional public education must create covenantal attachments via mediated identity, positive liberty, valorization, praxis, learningful conversations, social justice, and the capacity for judgment. It falls to traditional public educators to take action devoted to quality practice and dedicated to sharing this quality with stakeholders and policymakers. The necessity to take action to defend traditional public education in this way is illuminated by a number of formative conclusions that emerge from this discussion.

FORMATIVE CONCLUSIONS

Among the formative conclusions developed out of the data and perspectives in this book is the unending virtue in active continuous improvement of professional practices. Because the assault by plutocrats, policymakers, and free market proponents instills lower order cognition, segregation, my-side bias, and adult-centric policy in schooling, traditional public educators are committed to working on behalf of all students across the United States and with millions of colleagues to enrich function in traditional public education.

With this in mind, educators should undertake both model-of and model-for instruction based on research to orient classroom responses to student learning as educators employ points of practice to craft quality instruction. Organizing and prioritizing assumptions and responsibilities to implement quality instruction and reach transformative outcomes presents traditional public educators with the enduring and effective means necessary and sufficient to engage every US student with *how to think*.

A warning emerges as a next formative conclusion: any ideology focused on the destruction of traditional public education is an ideology intent on undermining democracy in the United States. The ideology of the free market as espoused by privatization proponents is diametrically opposed to fundamental precepts at the heart of actualizing successful democracy in the United States.

Free marketeers endorse policy and practice that is antithetical to equality; mechanisms restrict fundamental rights. Deliberate rejection of concepts found in the theoretical beacons from our nation's origin—concepts that US history shows are worthy but extremely difficult to enact day to day—demonstrates the cynical effect of the self-aggrandizing free market.

In addition, comprehensive traditional education's primary purpose facilitates the futures that all US students deserve but that are not yet accessible across all cohorts of American young people. The cognitive behaviors that fulfill individual dreams in balance with the public good, the social justice of valorization, and heuristic professional practice for continuous improvement—all are possible throughout traditional public education if a defense of professional practice thwarts the free market of schooling.

Engaging students' futures via professional practice oriented by points of practice and framed by the interwoven constructs of function allow traditional public educators the coherence and instructional power necessary to focus on a primary purpose and the outcomes of cognitive agency, wisdom, and successful intelligence. It is possible, further, to conclude formatively that the exceptionally difficult day-to-day professional practice in traditional public education operationalizes *how to think* for all students when colleagues establish points of practice to orient quality instruction. Points of practice maintain an eye-on-the-prize of quality professional practice in response to student learning on the journey to *how to think*.

Points of practice not only orient instruction, but they also provide touchstones for understanding how function intersects with human development as students learn. This ability to organize, prioritize, and guide professional practice provides traditional public educators with the means (instructional mapping) to mature *how to think* as one aspect of human development. Crafting a GPPS (Swennson, Ellis, and Shaffer, in press) to orient the mosaic artistry of professional practice provides colleagues with research-based means to realize the ends of greatest value from education and for the future of all US students.

TIRED YES, BUT NEVER TIRED OF SERVING STUDENTS

Because traditional public educators are tired of the societal vandalism wrought by marketeers, there is no need to offer apologies for adamant assertions about the worth of traditional public education. This discussion and its formative conclusions illustrate that educators know it is vital to mount a vigorous, data-based, and civil defense of function, quality, and primary purpose. This means, of course, that educators need to act on behalf all students for a return to full public and policy investment in the positive outcomes inherent in the professional practice of traditional public education.

The likelihood of a return to this focus depends, in part, on ending the internecine warfare generated by the effort to destroy traditional public education. As the authors abide by traditional public education colleagues and the need for a vigorous defense of professional practice, they can imagine an end to the current divisive state of educational affairs in the United States. The remainder of this concluding chapter, as a result, attends to whether the restoration of fiscal, political, and policy initiatives necessary to a robust future for traditional public education is possible.

CASTING A SPOTLIGHT ON ALL STUDENTS

A spotlight that dispels the shadows cast by free market schooling on a purposeful and quality traditional public education for all American students must be turned on. The capabilities, lived experience, and cognitive assets of all students must become the priority for education in the United States. *How to think* is the human right that free market schooling proponents ignore.

A collaborative engagement among educational professionals to prioritize the professional practices necessary and sufficient to lessons that teach *how to think* is a possible beginning for the end of the current civil war in US education. Collaboration can gather momentum from policies and statutes that establish *how to think* and continuous improvement as a funding priority in comprehensive American public education. Moreover, the glimmer of hope for the restoration of full support for all US students can be magnified if several additional actions are taken throughout the practice of education in America.

- *Collaborate.* Perhaps by remembering Albert Shanker's original thinking about what are now called *charter schools*, the leader of the National Association of Charter School Authorizers (NACSA) has called for US educators to curtail cacophonous conversations about quality in America's public schools.

    This entreaty eloquently notes that "our children, our educators, and our nation would be better served if ideologues on both sides turned down the rhetoric and encouraged all educators to work together more often" (Richmond, 2014). The implication in this plea is that the time has come for the rancorous dispute between TPS (traditional public schools) and PCS (public charter schools) to end.

A focus on a primary purpose in service to all US students is a starting point. To ensure meaningful collaboration, funding for traditional public education must be robust to ensure the end of rancor and the start of teamwork on a journey designed to craft *how to think* throughout American education.

- *Commemorate federal support.* Although Title I and special education funding from the federal government has long been less than students require, it's incumbent upon traditional public educators during collaboration with colleagues in choice schools to let their representatives know that sustaining and increasing existing support is necessary and appreciated (Leonor, 2018; Stratford, 2018a; Ujifusa 2018b). No longer should any perspective about education dedicate itself to the reduction of funding for these programs (Stratford, 2018a).

  The corollary to this vigilance is staying alert for attempts to siphon off funding from student-focused federal programs—which was attempted in the late 2010s to the tune of $1 billion out of Title I—to feed school choice (Leonor, 2018). When the US House and Senate expand the budget for programs that serve students and increase funding for policy riveted to *how to think* that brings both perspectives about education "on par," praise for elected representatives should be shared. However, it's vital to communicate how any increase in dollars for privatization hurts students in traditional public education (Stratford, 2018a) and that robust funding for all US students in public education must be nonnegotiable.

  The divisive funding shenanigans of some federal legislators need to be monitored. And the constructive, student-centered, budgetary efforts of other legislators should be saluted. For instance, federal legislators worked to scuttle an ill-disguised siphoning attempt by ideologues to budget "a $1 billion program designed to encourage open enrollment in districts" (Ujifusa, 2018b).

- *Unplug mechanisms masquerading as education.* State legislators hold the key to unplugging the education-free mechanisms that propel privatization. When traditional public school colleagues share information with policymakers about the devastating impact of mechanisms on students, an information flow is initiated with the objective of restoring full funding and support for professional practice and primary purpose in America's public schools.

  The more data shared about the debilitating effect of mechanisms and the more attention drawn to the ugly impact of funding shortfalls on children in traditional public education, the greater are the opportunities for altering the counterproductive division between perspectives about education in the United States. Communicating with policymakers and legislators allows dialogue to illuminate the importance of primary purpose and the impact of *how to think*.

- *Assert that successful intelligence is the right of every US student.* The failure to focus on what's best for all American students means that privatization ignores the present and future value of successful intelligence. Marketeers and policymakers fail abjectly when all US students in public schools cannot engage with higher order thinking skills, responsive cognition, cognitive agency, or *how to think* in the realm of what Sternberg (2008) refers to as the "Other 3 Rs."

  These three capacities—reasoning, resilience, and responsibility—illuminate a fraction of the cognitive agency and the public good arising from the pursuit of a primary purpose. It is time to call legislators and policymakers to the task of creating policy on behalf of all students in which them-versus-us mechanisms, inefficient efficiencies, and failing achievement are not allowed to impede the highest standards possible for teaching and learning.

- *Evidence that traditional public schools provide superior accountability.* The assumption that a free market provides adequate and meaningful accountability for all US students is overturned by reams of data.

  One of the many problems with free market thinking is that it "'embraces the principles of choice and autonomy while gutting accountability'" (Binelli, 2017, p. 9). Traditional public education colleagues must share data, share how they work to improve whatever the data indicates, and share how stealth-schooling runs away from accountability. The need for what can only be called *authentic accountability* is manifest throughout this discussion. Data that magnifies successful intelligence and how it develops within quality instruction needs to be the focus of all educators.

- *Remind legislators about the state constitution.* Numerous state constitutions establish uniform public education. In most cases, governance of traditional public education is the province of locally elected school boards or committees. The defense of traditional public education must emphasize that a state constitution's requirement for uniformity ought to be prioritized. Exemptions in statutes or regulations that establish or protect the primacy of self-interest and deny uniformity constitute an abrogation of this constitutional requirement (Long, 2018).

  State discrimination, thinking-as-rejection, segregation, inequitable access to state-funded schooling, larger per-pupil outlays for stealth-schooling—all demonstrate the lack of uniformity alive and well in the United States, to the detriment of countless students and their futures. Of equal concern is that unelected boards governing stealth-schools receive state funding and usurp the uniformity in democracy signified by an elected school board. The long and short of this denial of democracy is that free market governing boards rarely are accountable in any way to taxpayers (Long, 2018).

The dangers that ensue when these checks and balances are not in place must be illuminated. The practice of democracy in the United States, like the practice of any greater good, requires persistent implementation with fidelity to seek the ideals that, while difficult to attain, are the heart of liberty and justice for all. State legislators and parents/caregivers need to join traditional public educators to realize the guarantees provided in constitutions for all public schools. The same unity of purpose and direction is required to restore to all public schools the checks and balances of elected public education governance.

- *Stay in touch with state legislators.* State legislators need to hear from traditional public educators about ideas, issues, and concerns. Staying in touch begins with keeping track of education and the state legislature through educator networks, local newspapers, and news outlets.

  When information develops about a topic or a pending bill that advances free market schooling over traditional public education, individually written communications must be sent to legislators that indicate data-centered objections. When information develops about a topic or a pending bill that advances traditional public education, communications in support are needed. When educators stay in touch with local policymakers over time, there is a chance for a meaningful hearing if/when free market proponents seek to undermine the relationship between constituents, traditional public schools, democracy, and local legislators.

- *Enrich student learning.* A defense of traditional public education should rely on the strength of professional practice that yields cognitive capacity for balance between individual freedom and the public good inherent in each student's capacity for *how to think*.

  This defense lies not only in the various strategies shared throughout this book but also within data about student academic performance. After all is said and done, arguments in favor of the alleged differences and superiority of stealth-schooling evaporate in the face of overwhelming data showing that student achievement in traditional public education is equal to or better than that of students attending choice schools.

Because traditional public education produces achievement data no different from and often better than that of stealth-schools, traditional public education colleagues must share persistently that the free market treats education as if it is a commodity subject to manipulation by mechanisms that do not engage with student needs (Long, 2018). This fact puts the defense of traditional public education in a position it has long occupied but that has not been emphasized sufficiently: function in traditional public education is devoted to creating the cognitive wherewithal necessary for all students to freely choose their own bright futures in balance with the public good, which also establishes the robust freedoms of the social contract within US democracy.

Robust freedom for all students entails the banishment of a return on investment (ROI) from teaching and learning. ROI is a feature of the ideology of a free market and privatization that has no place in any reasoned discussion of education in the United States. ROI enters the conversation when privatization proponents launch tall tales about the dollars saved, the efficiencies created, and the students enlightened when ideological investments are made.

Unacknowledged by marketeers is that a return on investment in the corporate world assumes a one-way relationship between invested dollars and a monetary return that is counterproductive in the education world. Investment in products and services assumes a correspondence in the short term between monies invested and monies earned. A corporate product or service is, in the vast majority of cases, consigned to a limited function.

In traditional public education, learning *how to think* is neither a product nor a service. There is no direct, short-term, correspondence between investment and return on investment because the process of human adaptation requires continuous improvement that does not align with financial returns and efficiency of production. Banishing the corporate entanglement with ROI will allow educators and policymakers to focus on outcomes like successful intelligence and citizenship that are RTS (return to students) compatible.

How to think is the light given to students in traditional public education to guide their futures. The point of view shared throughout this book about the art and science of professional practice to engage students in responsive cognition, cognitive agency, and successful intelligence is supported by research that indicates that teaching and learning from this baseline allows students to outscore "other children even on the multiple-choice memory tests. . . . It enables children to capitalize on their strengths and to correct or to compensate for their weaknesses, and it allows children to encode material in a variety of interesting ways" (Sternberg and Grigorenko, 2004, p. 278).

AT THE END OF THE SCHOOL DAY

The health and well-being of democracy in the United States depends on the degree to which all citizens learn *how to think*. Free market theory undermines and shortchanges the capacity of all students to acquire responsive cognition and to establish cognitive agency. The reason traditional public education takes responsibility for cognitive agency is that all citizens "need to be taught to 'know and value what it means to participate in and be responsible for the care and improvement of our common and collective life'" (Westheimer and Kahne, 2003, p. 14).

Not only does free market theory abandon common and collective grounding for US society, but stealth-schooling advocates are unable to demonstrate improvement of student achievement alongside their related failure to "explain at the operational level how choice induces schools to improve student performance" (Carnoy et al., 2007, p. 3). Free market thinking denies the value of positive liberty in other ways:

- Ethical disengagement (Sternberg, Reznitskaya, and Jarvin, 2007) is a feature of privatization and the free market. The free market is anything but free for large cohorts of US students and families. The questionable ethics of privatization proponents apparently are assuaged by the calming effect of amorality in the free market.

  The negative effects of ethical disengagement constitute a clarion call to traditional public educators: social justice for and service to all students is the stock in trade of the profession and, thus, worth fighting for.

- The ideology of the free market prohibits consideration of "the other" and, thus, delays or denies the development of higher order thinking and mature stages of moral development and meaning-making. On the other hand, traditional public education and the pathway to *how to think* incorporates how "to construct and sometimes reconstruct knowledge from the point of view of others" (Sternberg, Reznitskaya, and Jarvin, 2007, p. 149).

  Denial and dissembling allow privatization proponents to smash other noses (figuratively) in the assertion of the primacy of self-interest. Survival of the fittest becomes survival of the chosen; the free market plays favorites and stealth-schooling aids and abets this despicable situation.

The deep values of human purpose that abide in the practice of traditional public education deserve not only a vigorous defense but, in the end, recognition as the value-added teaching and learning required for the success of US democracy. Instead of abiding by the forces and factors that push traditional public education out on a limb, the time has come to defend the worth of public education in no uncertain terms.

At the end of the day, educators are tired of the assault on both traditional public education and the professional practice of dedicated colleagues whose intellect, creativity, compassion, patience, and professionalism inspire *how to think* for children and young people throughout America. The defense of comprehensive traditional public education that matters most is composed of the ideas, actions, and policies dedicated to the proposition that society has an obligation to its children. This obligation is the provision of education that treats students as the most worthwhile investment possible in the greatest nation on earth.

Investing in ROI, investing in the free market, investing in mechanisms, investing in the abrogation of social justice—all countermand the potential of all students and, thus, obstruct the best of the human condition that could emerge from US democracy if all students benefited from a profound investment in *how to think*. Traditional public school colleagues must use the existing wide range of research, data, and/or other benchmarks of quality to evaluate, discuss, and demonstrate the worthwhile impact of professional practices on US students.

In addition to the numerous indicators of success discussed in this book, several benchmarks suggested by Strauss (2013) denote key elements of comprehensive traditional public education that must be defended: the presence of the arts in education, the extent of family engagement and satisfaction in traditional public education, the degree of teacher satisfaction and the extent to which teachers are supported, the great strength of diversity in traditional public education, and the impact of traditional public education on the future successes of graduates.

With so much data and with so many conceptual frameworks available, traditional public educators have resources readily available to defend the worth of professional practice while forestalling the desperation inherent in the free market of schooling.

As bad as the dollars-and-cents shortfall is for traditional public education, a more enduring problem is at hand. Most traditional public school educators do not realize that their greatest opponent is free market theory in schooling. Free market theory is not only responsible for funding shortfalls, but free market theory is also responsible for the ethos, the ideology, that engenders mechanisms and adult-centric priorities for American schooling.

Adherents of the free market of schooling promote less government as a greater good than traditional public education. Politicians, policymakers, and free market proponents rally to this vision and array significant obstacles in the path of traditional public education. And, with policymakers and politicians under the thrall of the free market's infatuation with less-is-more, support for quality professional practice deteriorates.

Among the many examples discussed throughout this book, the emphasis of free market advocates on standardized testing as the coin of the realm for evaluation of schools and teachers demonstrates the wide-ranging deterioration of purpose and quality in traditional public education. The clamor for implementing these tests in every state and tying the test scores to whether schools are closed or educators are fired ensures that inordinate amounts of instructional time are devoted to teaching to the test and that inordinate amounts of attention are paid to the fairy tales told by marketeers.

Traditional public educators experience the effects of free market theory daily. Too little, however, happens to organize and carry out self-defense among and on behalf of traditional public educators. As a result, the concepts, strategies, and proposals shared throughout this book are intended to augment and accelerate action dedicated to defending the purpose, funding, and outcomes of traditional public education.

Traditional public educators have the cognitive and research-based resources necessary to assert the purpose and quality of traditional public education. The time is right for action devoted to quality instruction, mediated identity, learningful conversations, *how to think*, positive liberty, and successful intelligence. Throughout each school day—as this discussion makes clear—*all* students in the United States deserve nothing less.

References

Abbott, L., and Costello, B. Who's on first? *YouTube*.
Abdulkadiroglu, A., Pathak, P. A., and Walters, C. R. (2015, December). School vouchers and student achievement: Evidence from the Louisiana Scholarship Program. Working Paper 21839. Cambridge, MA: National Bureau of Economic Research. Retrieved from http://www.nber.org/papers/w21839
Anderson, G. L., and Donchik, L. M. (2016). Privatizing schooling and policy making: The American Legislative Exchange Council and new political and discursive strategies of education governance. *Educational Policy (30)*2, 322–364. doi:10.1177/0895904814528794
Armstrong, T. (2018). *Multiple Intelligences in the Classroom*. Alexandria, VA: Association for Supervision and Curriculum Development.
Au, W., and Gourd, K. (2013, September). Why high stakes testing is bad for everyone, including English teachers. *The English Journal (103)*1, 14–19.
Bhattacharyya, S., Junot, M., and Clark, H. (2013). Can you hear us? Voices raised against standardized testing by novice teachers. *Creative Education (4)*10, 633–639. Retrieved from http://dx.doi.org/10.4236/ce.2013.410091
Bielke, D. (2017, June 15). WILL's faulty school voucher study cheered by other Bradley funded groups. *PRWatch*. Retrieved from http://www.prwatch.org/news/2017/06/13256/WILL-voucher-study-bradley-funded-groups
Binelli, M. (2017, September 15). Michigan gambled on charter schools. Its children lost. *New York Times*. Retrieved from https://nyti.ms/2xLofbr
Bloom, B. (Ed.) (1956). *Taxonomy of Educational Objectives: The Classification of Educational Goals*. New York: Longmans Green.
Bolsen, T. (2013). A light bulb goes on: Norms, rhetoric, and actions for the public good. *Political Behavior 35*, 1–20. doi:10.1007/s11109-011-9186-5
Boyland, L., and Ellis, J. (2015, Winter). The reasons that Indiana superintendents retire: Rhetoric and reality. *The AASA Journal of Scholarship and Practice (11)*4, 21–38.
Bracey, G. W. (2004). *Setting the Record Straight: Responses to Misconceptions about Public Education in the United States*. Portsmouth, NH: Heinemann
Bracey, G. W. (2009). *Educational Hell: Rhetoric vs. Reality*. Alexandria, VA: Educational Research Service.
Brooks, D. (2017, November 16). Our elites still don't get it. *New York Times*. Retrieved from https://nyti.ms/2jz2uZD
Brown, E. (2017, April 9). DeVos praises this voucher-like program. Here's what it means for school reform. *Washington Post*. Retrieved from https://www.washingtonpost.com/local/education/devos-praises-this-voucher-like-program
Brown, K. M. (2004). Leadership for social justice and equity: Weaving a transformative framework and pedagogy. *Educational Administration Quarterly (40)*1, 77–108. Retrieved from www.journals.sagepub.com/doi/10.1177/0013161X03259147
Brown, P. C., Roediger III, H. L., and McDaniel, M. A. (2014). *Make It Stick*. Cambridge, MA: The Belknap Press at Harvard University.
Brown v. Board of Education, 347 U.S. 483 (1954).
Burbank, M. J., and Levin, D. (2015). Community attachment and voting for school vouchers. *Social Science Quarterly (96)*5, 1169–1177. doi:1111/ssqu.12225
Butrymowicz, S. (2013a, August 22). Even in birthplace of charter schools, the grand experiment is at risk. *Time*. Retrieved from www.nation.time.com/2013/08/22/even-in-birthplace-of-charter-schools-the-grand-experiment-is-at-risk

Butrymowicz, S. (2013b, July 15). A new round of segregation plays out in charter schools. *The Hechinger Report.* Retrieved from www.hechingerreport.org/as-charter-schools-come-of-age-measuring-their-success-is-tricky

Cameron, K., and McNaughtan, J. (2014). Positive organizational change. *The Journal of Applied Behavioral Science (50)*4, 445–462. doi:10.1177/0021886314549922

Carey, K. (2017, March 2). DeVos and tax credit vouchers: Arizona shows what can go wrong. *New York Times.* Retrieved from https://www.nytimes.com/2017/03/02/upshot/arizona-shows-what-can-go-wrong-with-tax-credit-vouchers.html

Carey, K., and Harris, E. A. (2016, December 12). It turns out spending more probably does improve education. *New York Times.* Retrieved from http://nyti.ms2hfv3YM

Carnoy, M., Adamson, F., Chudgar, A., Luschei, T. F., and Witte, J. F. (2007). *Vouchers and Public School Performance: A Case Study of the Milwaukee Parental Choice Program.* Washington, DC: Economic Policy Institute.

Carr, S. (2012, December). In southern towns, "segregation academies" are still going strong. *The Atlantic.* Retrieved from https://www.theatlantic.com/national/archive/2012/12/in-southern-towns-segregation-academies-are-still-going-strong/266207

Cavazos, S. (2016, December 15). The broken promise of Indiana's online schools. *ChalkBeat.* Retrieved from http://www.chalkbeat.org/posts/in/2016/12/15/the-broken-promise-of-online-schools

Cavazos, S. (2017a, February 20). Lawmakers want to allow appeals before low-rated private schools lose vouchers. *ChalkBeat.* Retrieved from http://www.chalkbeat.org/posts/in/2017/02/20/lawmakers-want-to-allow-appeals-before-low-rated-private-schools-lose-vouchers

Cavazos, S. (2017b, May 10). Indiana officials opt to punish Hoosier Virtual and let it stay open. They told the long-failing school to do better. Again. *ChalkBeat.* Retrieved from https://chalkbeat.org/indiana-officials-opt-to-punish-hoosier-academy-virtual

Cavazos, S. (2018, January 4). Two Indiana Senate bills would tighten up rules for charter school oversight. *ChalkBeat.* Retrieved from https://chalkbeat.org/posts/in/2018/01/04/two-indiana-senate-bills-would-tighten-up-rules-for-charter-school-oversight

Chandler, M. A. (2015, August 26). Some D.C. charter schools get millions in donations; others, almost nothing. *Washington Post.* Retrieved from https://www.washingtonpost.com/some-charter-schools-get-millions-in-donations

Chetty, R., Reeves, R. V., and Pita, A. (2018, January 31). America's "lost Einsteins": The importance of exposing children to innovation. *Podcast.* Retrieved from https://www.brookings.edu/americas-lost-einsteins-the-importance-of-exposing

Chi, M. T. H., and Ohlsson, S. (2005). Complex declarative learning. In Keith J. Holyoak and Robert G. Morrison (Eds.) *Cambridge Handbook of Thinking and Reasoning,* 371–400. Retrieved from https://pdfs.semanticscholar.org/c0a0/b50e6aac35c513d7f4b2302b9e186aefb8bc8

Chubb, J. E., and Moe, T. M. (1988). Politics, markets, and the organization of schools. *American Political Science Review (82)*4, 1065–1087. Retrieved from http://links.jstor.org/sici

Chubb, J. E., and Moe, T. M. (1990). *Politics, Markets, and America's Schools.* Washington, DC: Brookings Institution.

Cochran-Smith, M., Shakman, K., Jong, C., Terrell, D. G., Barnatt, J., and McQuillan, P. (2009). Good and just teaching: The case for social justice in teacher education. *American Journal of Education (115)*3, 347–377. Retrieved from http://www.jstor.org/stable/10.1086/597493

Colombo, H. (2015, February 24). Big jump in voucher use for students who never tried public school. *ChalkBeat.* Retrieved from http://in.chalkbeat.org/2015/02/24/big-jump-in-voucher-use-for-students-who-never-tried-public-school

Colombo, H. (2017, June 26). Notre Dame study: Voucher students experienced math achievement losses. *Indianapolis Business Journal.* Retrieved from https://www.ibj.com/articles/print/64371-notre-dame-study-voucher-students-experienced-math-achievement-losses

Constitution of the United States. Retrieved from https://constitutioncenter.org
Cook, T., and Turner, K. (2015, June 7). Surprise charter school loan program raises new questions. *The Indianapolis Star*. Retrieved from https://www.indystar.com/story/news/politics/2015/06/07/surprise/28493699
Covaleskie, J. F. (2007). What public? Whose schools? *Educational Studies (42)*1, 28–43. doi:10.1080/00131940701399635
Cowen, J. M., Fleming, D. J., Witte, J. F., and Wolf, P. J. (2012). Going public: Who leaves a large, longstanding, and widely available urban voucher program. *American Educational Research Journal (49)*2, 231–256. doi:10.3102/0002831211424313
Cowen, J. M., Fleming, D. J., Witte, J. F., Wolf, P. J., and Kisida, B. (2013). School vouchers and student attainment: Evidence from a state-mandated study of Milwaukee's parental choice program. *The Policy Studies Journal (41)*1, 147–168. doi:10.1111/psj.12006
CREDO (Center for Research on Education Outcomes). (2009). *Multiple Choice: Charter School Performance in 16 States*. Stanford, CA: Stanford University.
CREDO. (2013). *National Charter School Study 2013*. Stanford, CA: Stanford University. Retrieved from http://credo.stanford.edu/documents/NCSS%202013%20Final%20Draft.pdf
Dawkins-Law, S. E. (2014). Why American needs a counterstory to "choice as the last civil right." *Sanford Journal of Public Policy (5)*2, 1–20. Retrieved from https://sites.duke.edu/sjpp/files/2014/05/Dawkins-Law
DeBray-Pelot, E. H., Lubienski, C. A., and Scott, J. T. (2007). The institutional landscape of interest group politics and school choice. *Peabody Journal of Education (82)*2–3, 204–230. Retrieved from https://gspp.berkeley.edu/assets/uploads/research/pdf/The_Institutional_Landscape_of_Interest_Group_Politics_and_School_Choice.pdf
Dewey, J. (1916). *Democracy and Education*. Retrieved from www.public-library.uk
Donheiser, J. (2017, July 18). What's ALEC? Ahead of Betsy DeVos's speech, here's which states earn the group's education policy praise. *Chalkbeat*. Retrieved from http://www.chalkbeat.org/posts/us/2017/07/18/whats-alec-ahead
Dunbar, F. (2018). Teaching mosaic: Putting together the pieces of interdisciplinary instruction. Retrieved from https://www.amle.org/A-Teaching-Mosaic-Putting-Together-the-Pieces-of-Interdisciplinary-Instruction
Eisner, E. W. (1979). *The Educational Imagination: On the Design and Evaluation of School Programs*. New York: Macmillan.
Elder, A. (2014, January–March). Do cyber charter schools help or hurt the educational system? *Penn State University Education News*. Retrieved from https://www.ed.psu.edu/educ/news/january-march-2014/cyber-charter
English, L. M., and Irving, C. J. (2012). Women and transformative learning. In Edward W. Taylor, Patricia Cranton, and Associates (Eds.) *The Handbook of Transformative Learning: Theory, Research, and Practice*, 245–254. San Francisco: Jossey-Bass.
Esposito, J., and Swain, A. N. (2009, Spring). Pathways to social justice: Urban teachers' uses of culturally relevant pedagogy as a conduit for teaching for social justice. *Perspectives on Urban Education*, 38–48. Retrieved from https://eric.ed.gov/?id=EJ838745
Finn, C. E. Jr., Hentges, C., Petrilli, M. J., and Winkler, A. (2009). *When Private Schools Take Public Dollars: What's the Place of Accountability in School Voucher Programs?* Washington, DC: Thomas B. Fordham Institute.
Fischer, B., and Peters, Z. (2016, March 8). ALEC continued to cash in on kids in 2015 and beyond. *PRWatch*. Retrieved from http://www.prwatch.org/news/2016/03/cashing-kids-172-alec-education-bills-2015
Fisher, D., and Frey, N. (2008). *Better Learning through Structured Teaching: A Framework for the Gradual Release of Responsibility*. Alexandria, VA: ASCD.
Fleming, D. J., Cowen, J. M., Witte, J. F., and Wolf, P. J. (2013). Similar students, different choices: Who uses a school voucher in an otherwise similar population of students? *Education and Urban Society (47)*7, 1–28. doi:10.1177/0013124513511268

Fraser-Burgess, S. (2012). Group identity, deliberative democracy and diversity in education. *Educational Philosophy and Theory (44)*5, 480–499. doi:10.1111/j.1469-5812.2010.00717.x

Freire, P. (1994). *Pedagogy of the Oppressed*. New York: Continuum.

Friedman, M. (1955). The role of government in education. In Robert A. Solo (Ed.) *Economics and the Public Interest*, 123–144. Retrieved from https://miltonfriedman.hoover.org/objects/58044//the-role-of-government-in-education

Fullan, M. (2001). *Leading in a Culture of Change*. San Francisco: Jossey-Bass.

Furman, G. (2012). Social justice leadership as praxis: Developing capacities through preparation programs. *Educational Administration Quarterly (48)*2, 191–229. Retrieved from https://eric.ed.gov/?id=EJ957152

Gabor, A. (2015, August 23). The myth of the New Orleans school makeover. *New York Times*, p. 3SR. Retrieved from https://www.nytimes.com/2015/08/the-myth-of-the-new-orleans-school-makeover

Gardner, H. (1983). *Frames of Mind: The Theory of Multiple Intelligences*. New York: Basic Books.

Goldstein, D. (2015). *The Teacher Wars: A History of America's Most Embattled Profession*. New York: Anchor Books.

Goldstein, D. (2017, April 11). Special ed school vouchers may come with hidden costs. *New York Times*. Retrieved from https://myti.ms/2onz9kO

Gorman, N. (2016, December 6). Betsy DeVos: 9 Facts that sum up everything you need to know. *education world*. Retrieved from www.educationworld.com/a_news/betsy-devos-9-facts-sum-everything-you-need-know-1764143159

Grant, C. A., and Gibson, M. L. (2013, February 5). "The path of social justice": A human rights history of social justice education. *Equity and Excellence in Education* 46(1), 81–99. doi:10.1080/10665684.2012.750190

Green, E. (2018, January/February). The charter-school crusader. *The Atlantic*. Retrieved from https://www.theatlantic.com/magazine/archive/2018/01/success-academy-charter-schools-eva-moskowitz/546554/

Green, E. L. (2017, April 28). Vouchers found to lower test scores in Washington schools. *New York Times*. Retrieved from https://nyti.ms/2pemnp7

Green, E. L. (2018a, March 9). After demanding local control, DeVos finds that it limits her influence. *New York Times*. Retrieved from https://nyti.ms/2GcOGvl

Green, E. L. (2018b, March 20). As DeVos faces Congress, officials say she hid plans to overhaul department. *New York Times*. Retrieved from https://nyti.ms/2u2HnDY

Hargreaves, A., and Fink, D. (2004). The seven principles of sustainable leadership. *Educational Leadership (61)*7, 8–13. Retrieved from www.ascd.org/leadership/The-Seven-Principles-of-Sustainable-Leadership.aspx

Hefling, K. (2017, October 30). How the Kochs are trying to shake up public schools, one state at a time. *POLITICO*. Retrieved from https://www.politico.com/story/2017/10/30/kochs-public-schools-shakeup-244259?cmpid=sf

Hefling, K. (2018a, January 26). States embrace new career and technical education policies; Ohio's virtual school quandary. *POLITICO'S Morning Education*. Retrieved from https://www.politico.com/morning-education/2018/01/26/states-embrace-new-career-and-technical-education-policies

Hefling, K. (2018b, March 6). Education Secretary Betsy DeVos gives education chiefs a little "tough love." *POLITICO'S Morning Education*. Retrieved from https://www.politico.com/newsletters/morning-education/2018/03/06/ed

Hefling, K. (2018c, April 8). Oklahoma walkout enters second week/Military groups push back against voucher-like bill. *POLITICO'S Morning Education*. Retrieved from https://www.politico.com/newsletters/morning-education/2018/04/09/oklahoma-walkout-enters-second-week-162751

Herron, A., and Fittes, E. K. (2017, November 26). Why more schools in danger of going broke. *The Indianapolis Star*, pp. 1A, 6A–8A.

Hess, F. M. (2010, Fall). Does school choice "work"? *National Affairs*, 35–53. Retrieved from www.nationalaffairs.com/publications/detail/does-school-choice-work

Higgins, C., and Knight Abowitz, K. (2011). What makes a public school public? *Educational Theory (61)*4, 365–380. doi:10.1111/j.1741-5446.2011.00409.x

Holyoak, K. J., and Morrison, R. G. (2005). Thinking and reasoning: A reader's guide. In Keith J. Holyoak and Robert G. Morrison (Eds.) *The Cambridge Handbook of Thinking and Reasoning,* 1–13. New York: Cambridge University Press.

Hostetler, K. (2003). The common good and public education. Book review. *Educational Theory (53)*3, 347–361. doi.10.1111/j.1741-5446.2003.00347

Hunter, M. (1982). *Mastery Teaching.* Thousand Oaks, CA: Corwin Press.

Hursh, D. (2007). Assessing No Child Left Behind and the rise of neoliberal education policies. *American Educational Research Journal (44)*3, 493–518.

Ignelzi, M. (2000). Meaning-making in the Learning and Teaching Process. *New Directions for Teaching and Learning 82*, 5–14. Retrieved from https://doi.org/10.1002/tl.8201

Indiana Constitution. (1851). *Constitution of the State of Indiana Article 8, Section 1.* As amended 2016. Retrieved from www.law.indiana.edu; www.iga.in.gov

Jennings, J. (2012). *Why Have We Fallen Short and Where Do We Go From Here?* Washington, DC: Center on Education Policy. Retrieved from https://eric.ed.gov/?id=ED528905

Jones, B. D., Thomas, H. F. III, and Wolfe, M. (2014). Policy bubbles. *Policy Studies Journal (42)*1, 146–171. Retrieved from https://doi.org/10.1111/psj.12046

Juarez, B. G., Smith, D. T., and Hayes, C. (2008). Social justice means just us white people: The diversity paradox in teacher education. *Democracy and Education (17)*3, 20–25. Retrieved from https://www.researchgate.net/234746632_Social_Justice_Means_Just_Us_White_People

Kahlenberg, R. D., and Potter, H. (2014, August 30). The original charter school vision. *New York Times.* Retrieved from https://www.nytimes.com/albert-shanker-the-original-charter-school-visionary.html

Kaufman, B. C. (2017, February 13). School vouchers bring more money to Catholic schools—but at a cost, study finds. *Notre Dame News.* Retrieved from http://news.nd.edu/news/school-vouchers-bring-more-money-to-catholic-schools-but-at-a-cost-study-finds

Kegan, R. (1980). Making meaning: The constructive-developmental approach to persons and practice. *The Personnel and Guidance Journal,* 373–380. doi:10.1002/j.2164-4918.1980.tb00416

Klein, R. (2017, December 26). Voucher schools championed by Betsy DeVos can teach whatever they want. Turns out they teach lies. *HuffPost.* Retrieved from https://www.huffingtonpost.com/entry/school-voucher-evangelical

Kohlberg, L., and Hersh, R. H. (1977). Moral development: A review of the theory. *Theory into Practice (16)*2, 53–59. Retrieved from http://links.jstor.org/sici?sici=0040-5841%28197704%2916%3A2%3C53%3AMDAROT%3E2.0.CO%3B2-%23

Komer, R. D., and Neily, C. (2007, April). School choice and state constitutions: A guide to designing school choice programs. *A joint publication of the Institute for Justice and The American Legislative Exchange Council.* Retrieved from https://eric.ed.gov/?id=ED514959

Krathwohl, D. R. (2002). A revision of Bloom's Taxonomy: An overview. *Theory Into Practice (41)*4, 212–218. Retrieved from https://www.depauw.edu/files/resources/krathwohl

Lalas, J. (2007, Spring). Teaching for social justice in multicultural urban schools: Conceptualization and classroom implication. *Multicultural Education.* Retrieved from http://eric.ed.gov/?id=EJ762417

Larson, R., and Angus, R. M. (2011). Adolescents' development of skills for agency in youth programs: Learning to think strategically. *Child Development 82*(1), 277–294. Retrieved from www.youthdev.illinois.edu

Lee, J. R. (1974). *Teaching Social Studies in the Elementary School.* New York: The Free Press.

References

Leo, U., and Wickenberg, P. (2013). Professional norms in school leadership: Change efforts in implementation of education for sustainable development. *Journal of Educational Change 14*, 403–422. doi:10.1007/s10833-013-9207-8

Leonor, M. (2018, March 22). Spending bill would give big boost to education. *POLITICO'S Morning Education*. Retrieved from https://www.politico.com/newletters/morning-education/2018/03/23/spending-bill-would-give-big-boost-to-education-147287

Levin, H. M. (2002). A comprehensive framework for evaluating educational vouchers. *Educational Evaluation and Policy Analysis (24)*3, 159–174. Retrieved from https://www.jstor.org/stable/3594163

Lezotte, L. W., and McKee, K. M. (2002). *Assembly Required: A Continuous School Improvement System*. Okemos, MI: Effective School Products.

Lithwick, D. (2018, February 28). They were trained for this moment. *Slate*. Retrieved from https://slate.com/news-and-politics/2018/02/the-student-activists-of-stoneman-douglas-high-demonstrate-the-power-of-a-full-education

Long, K. (2018). Indiana's charter schools: Taking a holistic approach to determine their constitutional legality. *Indiana Law Review (51)*3, 797–822.

Lubienski, C. (2013). Privatising form or function? Equity, outcomes and influence in American charter schools. *Oxford Review of Education (39)*4, 498–513. http://dx.doi.org/10.1080/03054985.2013.821853

Lubienski, C., Gulosino, C., and Weitzel, P. (2009). School choice and competitive incentives: Mapping the distribution of educational opportunities across local education markets. *American Journal of Education 115*, 601–647. Retrieved from http://www.jstor.org/stable/10.1086/599778

Lubienski, C., and Weitzel, P. (2008, March 1). The effects of vouchers and private schools in improving academic achievement: A critique of advocacy research. *Brigham Young University Law Review*, 447–485. Retrieved from https://www.researchgate.net/263045350

Marzano, R. J. (2007). *The Art and Science of Teaching*. Alexandria, VA: Association for Supervision and Curriculum Development.

Marzano, R. J., and Kendall, J. (1998). Awash in a sea of standards. *McREL.org*.

Maxwell, L. A. (2014, August 19). US school enrollment hits majority-minority milestone. *Education Week*. Retrieved from https://www.edweek.org/ew/articles/2014/08/20/01demographics.h34

Mayer, J. (2017). *Dark Money: The Hidden History of the Billionaires Behind the Rise of the Radical Right*. New York: Anchor Books.

Mayflower Compact. (nd). Retrieved from www.pilgrimhallmuseum.org

McKinney, J., and Shaffer, M. (2018, February). Special education in Indiana's voucher schools: What are parents giving up to gain choice? Paper presented at the meeting of the Eastern Educational Research Association, Clearwater Beach, FL.

Mead, R. (2016, December 14). Betsy DeVos and the plan to break public schools. *Daily Comment, New Yorker*. Retrieved from www.newyorker.com/news/daily-comment/betsy-devos-and-the-plan-to-break-public-schools

Mezirow, J. (1997). Transformative learning: Theory to practice. *New Directions for Adult and Continuing Education (74)*5, 5–12. doi:10.1002/ace.7401

Mezirow, J. (2000). Learning to think like an adult: Core concepts of transformation theory. In Jack Mezirow et al. (Eds.) *Learning as Transformation: Critical Perspectives on a Theory in Progress*, 3–33. San Francisco: Jossey-Bass. doi:10.1.1.463.1039

Michie, G. (2018, August 22). On the importance of mirrors for students (and teachers). *HuffPost*. Retrieved from https://www.huffingtonpost.com/gregory-michie/on-the-importance-of-mir_b_5604494

Molden, D. C., and Higgins, E. T. (2012). Motivated thinking. In Keith J. Holyoak and Robert G. Morrison (Eds.) *The Oxford Handbook of Thinking and Reasoning*, 390–412. Retrieved from https://www.researchgate.net/publication313563127_Motivated_Thinking

References

Moyers, B. (2014). Understanding the propaganda campaign against public education. *Perspectives*. Blog. Retrieved from http://billmoyers.com/2014/03/25/understanding-the-propaganda-campaign-against-public-education

NCTE (National Council of Teachers of English). (2014). *How Standardized Tests Shape and Limit Student Learning*. Retrieved from http://www.ncte.org/literacy/NCTEFiles/Resources/Journals/CC/0242-

Nichols, S., Glass, S., and Berliner, D. (2012, July). High-stakes testing and student achievement: Updated analyses with NAEP data. *Education Policy Analysis Archives (20)20*.

Nussbaum, M. (2011). Capabilities as fundamental entitlements: Sen and social justice. *Feminist Economics (9)2–3*, 33–59. Retrieved from https://doi.org/10.1080/1354570022000077926

Ogbu, J. U. (2004). Collective identity and the burden of "acting white" in black history, community, and education. *The Urban Review (36)1*, 1–32.

Patrick, J. J. (1999). The concept of citizenship in education for democracy. In Charles F. Bahmueller and John J. Patrick (Eds.) *Principles and Practices of Education for Democratic Citizenship: International Perspectives and Projects*. Retrieved from https://eric.ed.gov/?id=434866

PDK (Phi Delta Kappa). (2017). *Attitudes Toward the Public Schools*. Retrieved from http://www.pdkpoll.org

Petrilli, M., Finn, C., Hentges, C., and Northern, A. M. (2009). When private schools take public dollars: What's the place of accountability in school voucher programs? Washington, DC: The Fordham Foundation. Retrieved from https://edexcellence.net/publications/when-private-schools-take.html

Piaget, J. (1952). *The Origins of Intelligence in Children*. New York: International Universities Press.

Picchi, A. (2018, April 3). The 9 states where teachers have it worst. *MoneyWatch*. Retrieved from https://www.cbsnews.com/news/the-9-states-where-teachers-have-it-worst

Poole, M. S., and Van de Ven, A. H. (1989). Using paradox to build management and organization theories. *Academy of Management Review (14)4*, 562–578. doi:10.5465/AMR.1989.4308389

Popham, W. J. (1999). Why standardized tests don't measure educational quality. *Educational Leadership (56)6*, 8–15. Retrieved from www.eric.ed.gov.EJ581564

Quinn, D. D. (1989, September/October). The importance of teaching. *Royal Bank of Canada Newsletter (70)5*. Retrieved from http://tips.atozteacherstuff.com/449/quotes-for-teachers-if-a-doctor-lawyer-or-dentist

Ravitch, D. (2014). *Reign of Error: The Hoax of the Privatization Movement and the Danger to America's Public Schools*. New York: Vintage Books.

Ravitch, D. (2018, February 20). Indiana: GOP legislator proposes total privatization of Muncie School District. *Diane Ravitch's blog*. Retrieved from https://dianeravitch.net/2018/02/20/indiana-gop-legislator-proposes-total-privatization-of-muncie-school-district

Reay, D. (2004). "It's all about becoming a habitus": Beyond the habitual use of habitus in educational research. *British Journal of Sociology in Education (25)4*, 431–444. doi: 10.1080/0142569042000236934

Reisch, M. (2002). Defining social justice in a socially unjust world. *Families in Society: The Journal of Contemporary Human Services (83)4*, 343–354. Retrieved from https://www.researchgate.net/profile/Michael_Reisch/publication/273366488_Defining_Social_Justice_in_a_Socially_Unjust_World/links/56b89c6608ae3c1b79b2e1f2.pdf

Ressenger, J. (2018). NAEP scores flatline, achievement gaps persist. Millions of children are still left behind. Retrieved from https://janressenger.wordpress.com/2018/04/13/naep-scores-flatline-achievement-gaps-persist-millions-of-children-are-still-left-behind

Richmond, G. (2014, September 17). Collaborating, not competing: Charters as "laboratories of innovation." *Education Post*. Retrieved from http://educationpost.org/

collaborating-not-competing-charters-as-laboratories-of-innovation/#.
VHN9wWTF_AE

Rindermann, H., and Thompson, J. (2013). Ability rise in NAEP and narrowing ethnic gaps. *Intelligence (41)*6. Retrieved from https://www.sciencedirect.com/science/article/pii/S0160289613000895

Ringold, D. J. (2005). Vulnerability in the marketplace: Concepts, caveats, and possible solutions. *Journal of Macromarketing (25)*2, 202–214. doi:10.1177/0276146705281094

Ritchart, R., and Perkins, D. N. (2005). Learning to think: The challenges of teaching thinking. In Keith J. Holyoak and Robert G. Morrison (Eds.) *The Cambridge Handbook of Thinking and Reasoning*, 775–802. Retrieved from https://pdfs.semanticscholar.org/0e3b/9e4de493894a79f579155c09f0c4f006ac88

Rouse, C. E., and Barrow, L. (2008, August 6). School vouchers and student achievement: Recent evidence, remaining questions. *Annual Review of Economics (1)*1. Retrieved from http://www.annualreviews.org

Saint-Exupery, A. de. (1939). *Terre des Hommes*. Retrieved from www.antoinedesaintexupery.com/terre-des-hommes-1939

Saltman, K. (2016). Corporate schooling meets corporate media: Standards, testing, and technophilia. *Review of Education, Pedagogy, and Cultural Standards (38)*2, 105–123.

Santamaria, L. J. (2013). Critical change for the greater good: Multicultural perceptions in educational leadership toward social justice and equity. *Educational Administration Quarterly 50*(3), 347–91. doi:10.1177/00131161X13505287

Schmoker, M. J. (2006). *Results Now*. Arlington, VA: Association for Supervision and Curriculum Development.

Schneider, C. (2017, March 26). Verdict still out on vouchers. *The Indianapolis Star*, pp. 1A, 3A–4A.

Schneider, M. (2013, August 27). The time that ALEC got it right. *HuffPost*. Retrieved from https://www.huffingtonpost.com/mercedes-schneider/the-time-that-ALEC-got-it_b_3810847

Seaman, M. (2011). Bloom's Taxonomy: Its evolution, revision, and use in the field of education. *Curriculum and Teaching Dialogue 1 and 2*, 29–43. Retrieved from https://www.questia.com/library/bloom-s-taxonomy-its-evolution-revision-and-use

Shaver, J. P. (1997). The past and future of social studies as citizenship education and of research on social studies. *Theory and Research in Social Education (25)*2, 210–215. Retrieved from http://dx.doi.org/10.1080/00933104.1997.10505803

Shields, C. M. (2004). Dialogic leadership for social justice: Overcoming pathologies of silence. *Educational Administration Quarterly (40)*1, 109–32. doi:10:1177/0013161X03258963

Singer, S. (2017, February 18). Top 10 reasons school choice is no choice. *HuffPost*. Retrieved from https://www.huffingtonpost.com/entry/top-10-reasons-school-choice-is-no-choice_us_58a8d52fe4b0b0e1e0e20be3

Smith, V. (2018, May 1). Vic's statehouse notes #321. Retrieved from www.icpe2011.com

Sternberg, R. J. (2008). Excellence for all. *Association for Supervision and Curriculum Development (66)*2, 14–19. Retrieved from https://eric.ed.gov/?id=814361

Sternberg, R. J. (2017, December). Testing for better and worse. *Kappan*, 66–71.

Sternberg, R. J., and Grigorenko, E. L. (2004). Successful intelligence in the classroom. *Theory into Practice (43)*4, 274–280. Retrieved from www.tandfonline.com/doi/abs/10.1207/s15430421tip4304_5

Sternberg, R. J., Reznitskaya, A., and Jarvin, L. (2007). Teaching for wisdom: What matters is not just what students know, but how they use it. *London Review of Education (5)*2, 143–158. doi:10.1080/14748460701440830

Stitzlein, S. M. (2017, September 5). How to define public schooling in the age of choice? *Education Week*. Retrieved from http://www.edweek.org/ew/articles/2017/09/06/how-to-define-public-schooling-in-the.html

Stratford, M. (2018a, February 13). Budget fleshes out Trump higher ed agenda. POLITICO'S Morning Education. Retrieved from https://www.politico.com/newsletters/morning-education/2018/02/13/budget-fleshes-out-trump-higher-ed-agenda-103874

Stratford, M. (2018b, February 21). AP exam results show progress, but gaps still remain. POLITICO'S Morning Education. Retrieved from https://www.politico.com/newsletters/morning-education/2018/02/21/ap-exam-results-show-progress-but-gaps-still-remain-111822

Strauss, V. (2013, June 13). Why two reform movements—choice and accountability—have fallen short. Blog. *Washington Post.* Retrieved from www.washingtonpost.com/blogs/answer-sheet/wp/2013/06/13/why-two-reform-movements-choice-and-accountability-have-fallen-short

Strauss, V. (2015, August 25). One alarming map shows what today's school "reformers" are missing. *Washington Post.* Retrieved from https://www.washingtonpost.com/one-alarming-mapshows-what-todays-school

Swensson, J., Ellis, J., and Shaffer, M. (in press). *Unraveling Reform Rhetoric: What Educators Need to Know and Understand.* Lanham, MD: Rowman & Littlefield.

Thorsen, C., Gustafsson, J.-E., and Cliffordson, C. (2014). The influence of fluid and crystallized intelligence on the development of knowledge and skills. *British Journal of Educational Psychology (84)*4, 556–570. Retrieved from https://www.ncbi.nim.nih.gov/pubmed/24909645

Toppo, G., and Nichols, M. (2017, February 5). Wanted: Teachers of color. Even as U.S. schools are increasingly diverse, teaching force is still overwhelmingly white. *USA TODAY. The Indianapolis Star,* p. 3B.

Turner, C. (2016, December 7). School vouchers 101: What they are, how they work—and do they work? *National Public Radio.* Retrieved from https://www.npr.org/2016/school-choice-101-what-it-is-how-it-works-and-does-it-work

Ujifusa, A. (2018a, February 12). Trump seeks to cut education budget by 5 percent, expand school choice push. *Education Week's blogs.* Retrieved from www.blogs.edweek.org/trump_education_budget_2019_5_percent_cut_school_choice_push

Ujifusa, A. (2018b, March 23). President Trump signs spending bill that includes billions more for education. *Education Week's blogs.* Retrieved from http://blogs.edweek.org/edweek/president_trump_signs_spending_bill_increases_education

Ujifusa, A. (2018c, April 10). Military coalition tells congress not to raid federal budget for school choice. *Education Week's blogs.* Retrieved from http://blogs.edweek.org/edweek/military_coalition_tells_congress_not_to_raid_federal_budget_for_school_choice

Underwood, J., and Mead, J. F. (2012). A smart ALEC threatens public education. *Phi Delta Kappa International (93)*6, 51–55. Retrieved from http://www.edweek.org/ew/articles/2012/03/01/kappan_underwood.html?cmp=eml-contshr-shr-desk

USDOE (United States Department of Education). (2000, December). Monitoring school quality: An indicators report. Washington, DC: National Center for Education Statistics. Retrieved from https://nces.ed.gov/pubs2001/2001030

Villegas, A. M. (2007). Dispositions in teacher education: A look at social justice. *Journal of Teacher Education 58*(5), 370–380. doi:10.1177/0022487107308419

Walsh, M. (2017, October 12). "Backpack full of cash" documentary fuels controversy over school choice. *Education Week.* Retrieved from http://blogs.edweek.org/edweek/education_and_the_media/2017/10/backpack_full_of_cash_film_packs_controversy_over_portrayal_of_school_choice

Westheimer, J., and Kahne, J. (2003). Reconnecting education to democracy: Democratic dialogues. *Phi Delta Kappan (85)*1, 9–14. Retrieved from https://eric.ed.gov/?id=EJ674581

Index

ALEC. *See* American Legislative Exchange Council
AYP. *See* Adequate Yearly Progress
ESSA. *See* Every Student Succeeds Act of 2015
NAEP. *See* National Assessment of Educational Progress
NCLB. *See* No Child Left Behind

academic achievement, 65, 98, 146
academic performance, 8, 66, 112
accountability, 89, 90
Adequate Yearly Progress (AYP), 101
American Legislative Exchange Council (ALEC), 13, 93, 103, 110, 112, 113, 120, 127

balance, 18
Bloom, Benjamin, 10, 54

charter schools, 9, 11, 109, 114, 118, 126
continuous improvement, 22, 23, 75, 80, 131
covenantal attachment, 18, 67

democracy, 15, 16, 18, 23, 25, 47, 63, 67, 72, 144, 146
Dewey, John, 13, 15, 25, 139

education, 16; choice, 27, 89, 112, 114, 115, 120
Every Student Succeeds Act of 2015 (ESSA), 99

free market, 146; funding, 9, 131, 132; mechanisms, 4, 7, 12, 26, 29, 65, 68, 138, 142; schooling, 1, 4, 7, 53, 59, 60, 63, 111, 114, 118, 127, 137, 138, 141, 147; theory, 1, 2, 7, 26, 61, 137
Freire, Paulo, 85

Ft. Wayne Community Schools, 24
Function, 39, 40, 42, 50, 70, 131

habits of mind, 31, 32, 45
how to think, 10, 16, 23, 44, 47, 49, 73, 75, 76, 80, 99, 104, 138, 145

identity, 70, 72, 73, 75, 81, 85, 139
instruction, 42, 43, 50, 77, 109, 139
intelligence, 30, 31, 32, 36; successful, 36, 41, 43, 69, 143

Marjory Stoneman Douglas High School, 83
marketeers, 2, 9, 26, 59, 67, 91, 114, 140, 145
meaning-making, 69, 70
mediated identity, 69, 74, 76, 78, 81, 84, 86
my-side bias, 60, 120

National Assessment of Educational Progress (NAEP), 97, 98
No Child Left Behind (NCLB), 92, 93, 97, 101

points of practice, 40, 50, 51, 52, 140
praxis, 84, 87
privatization, 1, 8, 12, 47, 60, 61, 64, 65, 110, 113, 116
public education: funding, 127, 128, 134; moral purpose, 19; primary purpose, 6, 25, 117, 142; traditional, 2, 5, 10, 11, 13, 17, 23, 29, 39, 45, 55, 67, 72, 82, 87, 106, 119, 125, 127, 129, 141, 147
public good, 18, 86, 117, 143

Ravitch, Diane, 93, 105, 123
reform, 2, 12, 114

segregation, 66
social justice, 16, 76, 82, 84, 86, 87
standards, 93, 94, 102, 104
standardized testing, 8, 53, 89, 94, 95, 96, 102, 104, 106, 147
stealth-schooling, 11, 12, 53, 64, 65, 68, 111, 114, 133
students, 74, 83, 102, 143, 145

transformative learning theory, 19

virtual schooling, 113
vouchers, 11, 27, 109, 118

About the Authors

Jeff Swensson, PhD
Dr. Jeff Swensson served for forty-five years as an educator in K–16 public education. His extensive experience in diverse school communities as a teacher, school leader, district leader, and assistant professor gives him a perspective enriched by innumerable opportunities for learningful conversations, instructional leadership, and continuous professional improvement. His scholar/practitioner interests include school leadership, quality school practices, and traditional public education. He is the author of peer-reviewed articles, a newspaper column, and thank-you notes to countless colleagues whose expertise makes a profound difference for students.

John Ellis, PhD
Dr. John Ellis served public education across Indiana as a teacher, assistant principal, principal, assistant superintendent, superintendent, and as executive director of the Indiana Association of Public School Superintendents for more than forty-three years. He graduated from Ball State University with a BA, a master's, and EdS in education before earning his PhD from Indiana State University. As a superintendent, he wrote a weekly newspaper education column. He is the author and coauthor of published peer-reviewed articles focusing primarily on school finance, the school superintendency, and the impact of politics on education.

Michael Shaffer, EdD
Dr. Michael Shaffer is assistant professor of educational leadership at Ball State University. He currently teaches politics, school finance, school facilities, and human resources and the central office administrator. Dr. Shaffer has been very involved in writing in support of traditional public education. He has also traveled extensively, speaking on the topic of literacy and the process of getting boys to read. Prior to coming full time to Ball State, Dr. Shaffer served in a number of schools and school districts, both public and private, as a principal at all levels and as an assistant superintendent.

www.ingramcontent.com/pod-product-compliance
Lightning Source LLC
Chambersburg PA
CBHW022014300426
44117CB00005B/188